Rapid Memory in 7 Days

Also Available in the Excell-erated Skills Series from Perigee Books

RAPID MATH IN 10 DAYS
RAPID READING IN 5 DAYS
RAPID WRITING IN 6 DAYS

RAPID Memory in 7 Days

The Quick-and-Easy Guide to Better Remembering

Joan Minninger, Ph.D.,
and Eleanor Dugan

A Perigee Book

A Perigee Book
Published by The Berkley Publishing Group
200 Madison Avenue
New York, NY 10016

Book design by Irving Perkins Associates, Inc.

Cover design by Bob Silverman, Inc.

Interior illustrations by David Dugan

The cartoon that appears on p. 170 is used courtesy of Tribune Media Services, Inc.

First Perigee edition: September 1994

Published simultaneously in Canada.

Library of Congress Cataloging-in-Publication Data

Minninger, Joan.
Rapid memory in seven days : the quick-and-easy guide to better remembering / Joan Minninger and Eleanor Dugan.
—1st Perigee ed.
p. cm.
Includes bibliographical references.
ISBN 0-399-52130-5 (alk. paper)
1. Mnemonics. I. Dugan, Eleanor. II. Title.
BF385.M862 1994
153. 1′4—dc20 94-6937
CIP

Printed in the United States of America

10 9 8 7 6 5 4 3 2 1

To Jill Coogan

CONTENTS

TO THE READER

This book is the result of a close collaboration between two authors, even though you will find most experiences described in the first person singular, "I." We thought of using the editorial and factual "we," but soon saw that it was awkward and seemed too impersonal. So "I" often means "we," except that the first-person therapy and seminar stories are by me, Joan Minninger, and the first-person stories involving the arts are by me, Eleanor Dugan.

HOW TO USE THIS BOOK

Rapid Memory in 7 Days is an instruction manual about using and enjoying your amazing memory to its fullest potential. The book is divided into seven sections. You can choose to cover one section every day for a week or you can select a more leisurely approach, doing only one or two exercises at each sitting. Feel free to jump ahead to a section that interests you, to double back, even to skip material that doesn't seem relevant to your needs at the moment. You can always change your mind later.

Surviving in today's Information Age can often seem overwhelming. *Rapid Memory in 7 Days* shows you how to cope with the constant onslaught of facts and figures we all must deal with every day. You'll learn ancient and modern systems for storing and recalling information, plus dozens of practical how-tos for everyday memory tasks. You'll read about the latest memory experiments and discoveries. Most important, you'll develop a greater appreciation for your extraordinary memory capacity, how it works, what enhances it, and how to overcome those pesky memory blocks that seem to hit at the most inopportune moments. You'll hone your memory for greater speed, efficiency, and confidence.

Rapid Memory in 7 Days

DAY 1

Your One-Minute Memory Manager

WHAT YOU'LL LEARN IN THIS CHAPTER

- A "peg system" that makes it easy to memorize a list of ten things in less than a minute and hundreds of things in less than an hour by attaching them to a structure you already know. You can recall them anytime you want, backward or forward, even five years later.

You want to remember millions of things? That's easy. Fortunately you already do.

But to remember one *specific* thing at the precise moment you choose to recall it is a bit harder. Memories can be infuriating, enchanting things that sometimes need coaxing, tricking, and a bit of housekeeping. This book is going to show you a number of proven ways to cope with information. Some of them require you to change the comfortable way you've been doing things, and some of them require effort.

Before you get discouraged, try the same sales gimmick that many diet programs offer—a fast start with quick results. Let's hit the ground running with an easy-to-learn, foolproof memory system that never lets you down. It can get you through speeches, exams, interviews, and it's also great for impressing people at parties.

I've been demonstrating this memory trick for more than twenty years.

In my workshops I start participants with twenty objects, but in this chapter, we'll start with an easy ten. (As soon as you've mastered these first ten, I'll show you how to expand your memorized list to twenty, fifty, even a hundred objects, still taking only a few seconds to fix each item in your memory.)

In my seminars, people in the audience call out any twenty random objects within a two-minute time period, and then I immediately repeat them back in any order. You may find this even more remarkable when I tell you that my inborn memory ability is probably no better than yours. It's precisely *because* I have trouble keeping track of things that I turned to memory tricks and strategies.

Of course, any trick is simple, once you know how it is done. As soon as I have explained the process, everyone in my audiences finds it just as easy to do, and so will you.

YOUR FIRST MEMORY TRICK: THE PEG SYSTEM

Here's how your *One-Minute Memory Manager* works. You take the things you want to recall without referring to notes—facts for a test, key points of a presentation, arguments in favor of a raise during a meeting with your boss, jokes or gossip you'd like to repeat after a gathering—and you attach each new thing to a place in a structure you already know. You create a mental "peg" to hang it on. For my demonstration, I use something you probably carry with you at all times—your body.

1. The top of your head

Make a mental picture of the first thing you want to remember. Then imagine that it is on top of your head, or it is stuck in your hair, or your hair has turned into this thing. Or the object you want to remember is dripping down over your face. Feel this object digging into your scalp. Is it hot, cold, wet, dry, pleasant, painful? Imagine the expressions on people's faces when they see it there.

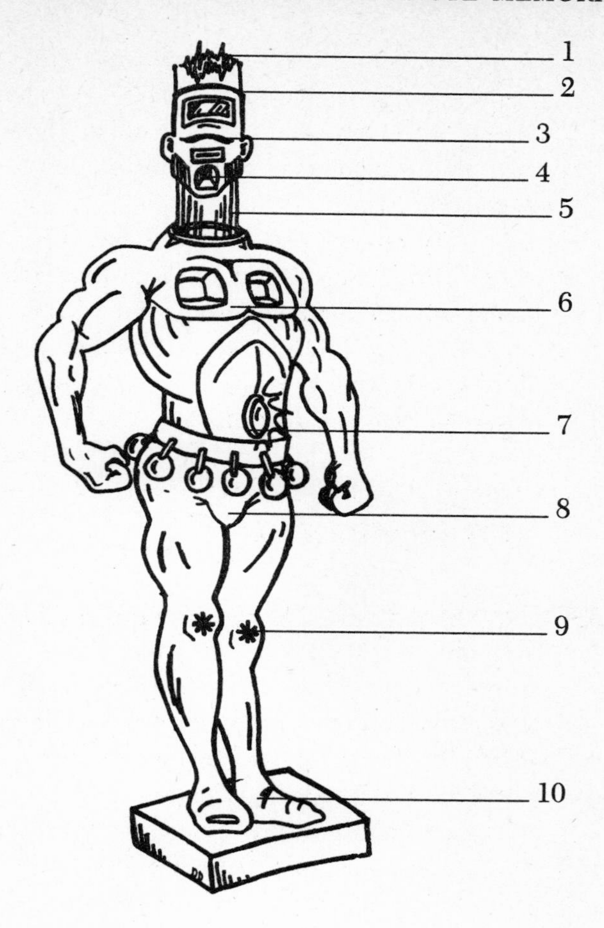

2. Your forehead

Your forehead has turned into a giant advertising sign for the second thing. See the slightly peeling sheets of gaudily printed paper on the billboard and feel them being stuck to your skin. Or the object is depicted by a huge electric sign, its loops and swirls pressed into the flesh of your forehead. Or your forehead has become a giant TV screen with the TV character you love or hate most shouting about this thing, holding it up, thrusting it at the camera. How do you feel about this? (Emotions fix memories!)

3. Your nose

Your nose has stretched out several feet, like Pinocchio's, and pierces this third billboard object. Or this thing is perched on your huge nose. Or your nose is a hose gushing this thing. Or the thing is growing out of your nose, astonishing onlookers. (Notice that you skipped the eyes. They offer such powerful imagery that I've found people often get them confused with the object itself.)

4. Your mouth

It's a tunnel with the fourth item driving in or pouring out. Or your teeth or tongue become the object. Taste it, imagine how it would feel to chew it or kiss it. Are others amused? Horrified?

5. Your throat

Your throat is a transparent glass cylinder, like a jewelry-store window, and your fifth object is displayed there. Pinpoint spotlights are focused on the object, which glitters in the intense light. Uniformed guards may be needed to protect it. What kind of people are lined up to press their noses against the glass? What are they saying? Are you laughing at them or applauding their perceptiveness?

6. Your chest

You have two of the sixth object, stored on your chest like lungs. Imagine a brassiere made out of this object. Or a giant earth mother suckling her young with this substance. Or a he-man chest with this substance forming the chest hair or entangled in it.

7. Your belly button

Object number seven is fastened there, glittering, blazing, blinking on and off. How does it look? Is it attached by an umbilical cord or is it growing directly out of your navel? Or does it form a belt around your waist with an O-shaped buckle that reveals your navel?

8. Boy or girl?

Your hips—or anything in the area between navel and knees—offer many possibilities. Numerous versions of item eight could hang on a hip belt. What do they sound like as you walk? Or a wallet or runner's pouch could be stuffed with it. Or you could be sitting in this substance. What does it feel like? (Yuck?) Or this object might be involved in a bodily function. You'll never forget this object, once you've made the connection.

9. Your knees

You are kneeling on the ninth object. What is the sensation? Is it delightful? Dreadful? Really feel it. Does it hurt? What does the weight of your body do to this object? Crush it? Wrinkle it? Do you leave knee-shaped indents in it?

10. Your feet

You are standing on the tenth object. What does it feel like? What are your feet doing to the object? Do you want to stamp up and down on it or stand as still as possible? Is it hot or cold? Wet or dry? Picture the reactions of people you know if they saw you walking down the street wearing shoes made of this.

Those are ten always-available memory pegs, your portable *One-Minute Memory Manager* system. Since you need only a few seconds to "fix" an object to each peg, you can easily notice, store, and retrieve—painlessly memorize—ten objects in less than a minute.

HOW TO REMEMBER CONCEPTS

Remembering nonsensical lists of objects—tennis racquet, elephant, cabbage—has little to do with real life. Remembering errands and what to buy at the store does. What if the things you want to remember aren't *things*? What if they are ideas? Turn the ideas into physical images and then hang that image on one of your pegs. Some possibilities are:

liberty—Statue of Liberty
oppression—whips, jail cell door
freedom—bird flying out of cage
taxation—tax forms
mental illness—straitjacket
happiness—smiling clown, bluebirds, party whistles
sadness—crying face, weeping willow tree
death—tombstone
birth—baby rattle, stork
environment—pine tree
pollution—garbage, black stinky goo

Choose images that immediately come to mind, things from your own experiences. The more you personalize your images, the more memorable they will be.

When I make a speech, I use images of objects to trigger my memory of concepts. Let's say I want to discuss the three kinds of memory blocks—emotional, mechanical, and physical. On the appropriate peg, depending on where this information comes in my speech, I attach

Emotional memory blocks—Greek tragedy and comedy masks carved on a marble block. (The "block" triggers the sequence.)

On the next peg are

Mechanical memory blocks—a jumble of cogs and wheels.

And the next has

Physical memory blocks—one of those horrible Physical Education uniforms I had to wear as a child.

As I make a speech, I can surreptitiously keep my "place" in my sequence of body pegs with gestures, lightly touching my nose, throat, or waist if need be, digressing as much as I want on any point, but always coming back to where I left off before going on to the next one. This way I don't leave out important things I wanted to say.

Philosophical, political, or scientific ideas can all be turned into objects. What if you want to remember whether the Pennsylvanian period was part of the Paleozoic or Mesozoic Era? (Or rather, what if some teacher wants you to remember something long enough to pass a test on a subject you care nothing about? If you were truly excited about geology or paleontology, you'd have known your Cambrian period from your Silurian as a child and could be using *them* as pegs for remembering other things.)

In addition to creating visual equivalents of abstract concepts, you can choose an object that *sounds* like the concept and so will trigger your memory. For example, "Pennsylvania" might be represented by the Liberty Bell (which is in Philadelphia) or by a pen (sounds similar); "Paleozoic" by a pail (similar sound); and Mesozoic could become a clump of mesquite or an ample mezzo-soprano opera singer (similar sound) or a dinosaur (existed in this period).

As you're probably starting to realize, most memory gimmicks are quite ridiculous. That's exactly why they are memorable.

Throughout this book you are going to find quizzes and games under the heading:

CHECK THIS OUT

They are intended to show you how your memory works, not to offer opportunities for feeling good or bad about your answers. Thus there is no formal scoring, only suggestions for what to notice about your answers.

CHECK THIS OUT

Practice Your New Trick

First, fix the ten body pegs in your mind. Repeat them quickly to yourself. If you miss one, go back and do it again and again until they are automatic. Take a few minutes to do this if necessary. Your success depends on being totally fluent with your body-part pegs, because if you can't recall the pegs, you won't be able to recall what's on them. Then get a friend to make a list of any ten objects and call them out to you, one at a time. Repeat the name of the object and fix it firmly to its peg. Then say, "Next." Don't rush yourself, although you'll probably come up with a strong mental image within a few seconds. When you've locked in all ten things, recite the list, top to bottom, or bottom to top.

If you're alone, choose ten things you'd really like to remember and write them down below. Work quickly but casually, with no sense of pressure.

1. Top of head ________________
2. Forehead ________________
3. Nose ________________
4. Mouth ________________
5. Throat ________________
6. Chest ________________
7. Navel ________________
8. Boy or girl? ________________
9. Knees ________________
10. Feet ________________

When you're through, set the list aside and recall the things, backward or forward. Check the accuracy of your answers. How did you do?

RECALLING FIVE YEARS LATER

Using the body-peg system is a good quick way to "cram" for a test, but what if you want to recall the information later but don't want to bother actually "learning" it, like the steps for operating a piece of equipment you rarely use? You do it the same way you get to Carnegie Hall: practice! Run down your body once a week for a month or so and then once a month, then once every few months. As long as you don't replace the information on your body pegs with other information ("retroactive interference"), you'll always be able to call it back, to *remember* it.

RULES FOR PEG SYSTEMS

But what if there are several sequences that you want to be able to recall over a period of months or years? Simply store each on a different set of pegs. The orators of ancient Greece—perhaps borrowing a technique from those who were ancient to *them*—used a simple system to remember the key points of their speeches. They associated each with a room of their homes. Then they mentally walked in their front door and moved from room to room, retrieving each idea in turn.

You can use any series of things to make a peg system as long as they are totally familiar to you and offer potential for strong visual connecting images: your home, landmarks on your way to work, your workplace, any series of things connected with your family or hobby or travels.

There are only two rules for choosing pegs:

1. They must be totally different from the things you want to remember. (You can't effectively "attach" furniture to furniture, mountains to mountains, or books to books.)
2. Remembering them in sequence should be completely effortless, almost second nature. You don't want to be straining to remember the pegs as well as what's attached to them.

WARNING: Any memory system you choose to use must suit your needs and temperament or you won't use it. If the peg system seems difficult or confusing, go on to the next chapter and find another system more to your liking. Remember that your memory belongs to *you* and so do your memory tricks. You can be as conventional or as absurd as you like because no one else will know—unless you slip up and address Mrs. Colliface as "Mrs. Lassie."

REMEMBERING ANOTHER FIFTY THINGS

Right now you can easily remember a million things in a specific order because of a simple system you learned in school. It's called counting.

You can probably count from 1 to 1,000,000 or even higher with no difficulty. Numbers *can* be used in the peg system, and some ways to do this are introduced in Chapter 5. However, most people do better with visual images.

Once you've mastered the first ten body pegs, go on to create additional sets of peg units. They will let you recall an almost unlimited number of items, provided:

- One set of pegs leads you naturally to the next set.
- The pegs within each set aren't too similar to the pegs in other sets.
- You enjoy using this particular trick. (There are lots of others.)

An excellent source of pegs is easily found in your own home. Imagine walking in the front door and entering each room in sequence, attaching what you want to memorize to major pieces of furniture. Don't despair if you live in a studio apartment. There are still lots of natural peg sequences in your life.

Working in subsets of five or ten pegs is easiest for accounting purposes. Once you've used up the ten pegs of your body, you will probably progress in units of five. That's because very few rooms have ten important features. (If you have such a room, by all means use it!)

Choose five important objects as memory pegs in the first room you come to, then five more from the next room. If the rooms don't offer useful pegs, go on to other rooms in your house or business. You can also use areas that are not technically rooms, such as patios, gardens, garages—anyplace that you know by heart and that is full of immobile, highly suggestive *things*.

Start at the doorway and mentally go clockwise around the first room, attaching each item to a major stationary object. When you hit five, stop and go on to another room.

Potential Pegs Check List

Here is a checklist of some possibilities. Put a check next to the ones that immediately resonate with images for you.

Living room

[ ] **Couch:** Your sofa is smeared or upholstered with this. Or the object is sinking deep into the cushions. Or the cushions are made of it. Do you want to sit down?

[ ] **Lamp:** The light bulb has been replaced by this or the shade or lamp base is made of it. Or the rays of light emanating from the lamp are actually bars of this substance. You are astonished!

[ ] **Television:** One TV has turned into a wall of screens, each with a flickering picture of this item. Imagine a commercial for it. Or this thing is glued to or running down the TV screen.

[ ] **Bookcase:** Hundreds of this object are neatly lined up on the shelves. Take one out and try to open it to read. Or they are tumbling out onto the floor. What are they doing to the carpet?

[ ] **Stereo:** Your object has been compressed into a disk or cassette shape and you are trying to play it. What sounds come out? How does it look revolving on the turntable? Or when you hit the eject button, this item pours out onto the floor.

[ ] **Fireplace:** It's burning! Do you try to pull it out? Or throw on more wood? What kind of smoke is it giving off? Or is it putting out the fire? Does your object form the mantel of the fireplace or the fire tongs?

[ ] **Telephone:** You reach for the receiver and find your object in your hand. How do you feel? Do you drop it immediately?

[ ] **Table:** It is stacked high on the table or dribbling off it or it has become the table itself.

Kitchen

[ ] **Stove:** The stove is burning it. It sits in quadruplicate on all four burners, bubbling, steaming. It is melting all over the stove and down onto the floor. The oven door bursts open and this thing emerges, puffed up with the heat like a yeasty loaf of bread.

[ ] **Sink:** Your sink is splashing water all over it. Or the article is pouring out of the faucets. It is sliding away down the drain as you try to grab it, or maybe it forms a giant sink stopper. Or the faucets are each made of this object. Feel them as you try to turn them.

[ ] **Refrigerator:** It is frozen in the ice trays, dozens of tiny, glittering

cubes. Or it gushes out of the ice-water dispenser. Open the door and there it is, huddled shivering in the corner. It is covered with icicles.

[ ] **Toaster:** Your object is flattened to fit in the toaster slots. Watch it pop up. What happens when you slather it with butter and jam?

[ ] **Food processor:** What happens when you put this object in the blender or processor? Whip it, mince it, stuff it down the tube and listen to what happens. Imagine pouring it out into elegant dessert goblets.

[ ] **Trash compactor:** Plop this item in and picture what happens to it as it is compressed. Watch it walk out in its new shape, with two little legs sticking out so it looks like a character in a cartoon.

[ ] **Electric can opener:** You open a big can and dozens of this thing pop out like canned peas. Or this item is glued to or drizzling down the can opener.

[ ] **Cabinets:** Open the doors and jump back as hundreds of this thing tumble onto the floor. It is stacked or crammed or lurking behind the doors. Or it has stuck itself all over the dishes or cereal boxes inside. Imagine trying to set the table with flattened versions of this thing. If this is a cabinet for a broom or an ironing board, imagine that the broom straws have been replaced by this thing or that you are trying to iron it on the ironing board.

Bathroom

[ ] **Tub:** This object is soaking or floating or swimming in a tub full of water. Do you want to climb in with it? What does water do to it? Or it fills the tub by itself.

[ ] **Toilet:** Push the handle and watch it flush down the toilet. Or imagine sitting on a toilet seat made of this thing.

[ ] **Toilet paper dispenser:** It is pressed into a ribbon of flat squares that unreel from the roll. Would it be squeezably soft?

[ ] **Towel racks:** Your object is draped over the towel bars like melted Salvador Dali watches. Reach for it to dry your hands and feel your surprise.

[ ] **Clothes hamper:** It is stuffed in among your clothes. Will it hurt them? Or it forms the lid of the hamper, snapping at you, leering, frightening, amusing you.

Bedroom

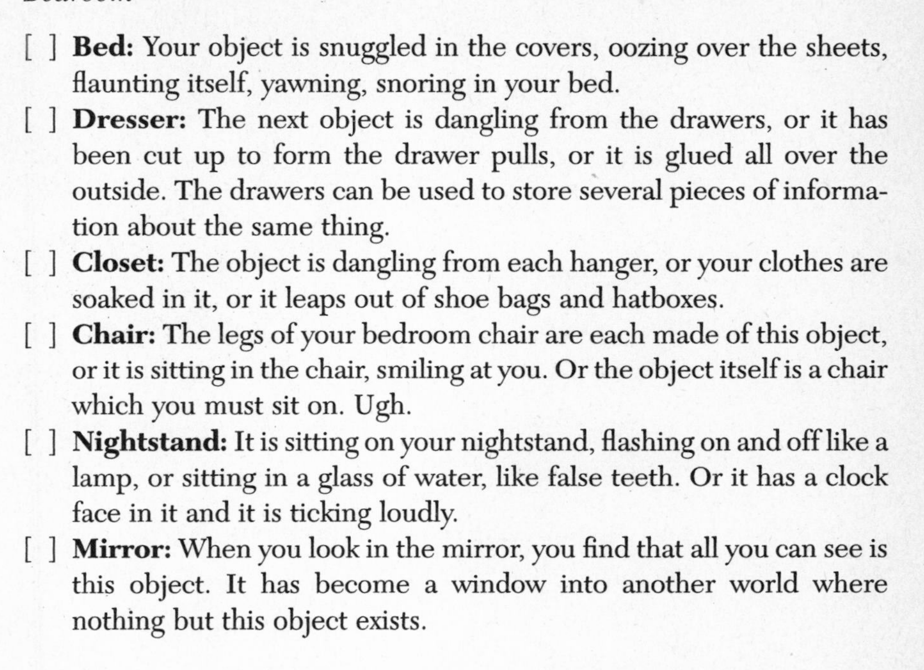

[ ] **Bed:** Your object is snuggled in the covers, oozing over the sheets, flaunting itself, yawning, snoring in your bed.

[ ] **Dresser:** The next object is dangling from the drawers, or it has been cut up to form the drawer pulls, or it is glued all over the outside. The drawers can be used to store several pieces of information about the same thing.

[ ] **Closet:** The object is dangling from each hanger, or your clothes are soaked in it, or it leaps out of shoe bags and hatboxes.

[ ] **Chair:** The legs of your bedroom chair are each made of this object, or it is sitting in the chair, smiling at you. Or the object itself is a chair which you must sit on. Ugh.

[ ] **Nightstand:** It is sitting on your nightstand, flashing on and off like a lamp, or sitting in a glass of water, like false teeth. Or it has a clock face in it and it is ticking loudly.

[ ] **Mirror:** When you look in the mirror, you find that all you can see is this object. It has become a window into another world where nothing but this object exists.

You can continue with your yard, office, or favorite store. Besides furniture you can also use windows and doors if they open onto something unique. A lake or mountain seen from a window could become your object. A staircase or Murphy bed behind a door offers succulent memory-peg possibilities.

Your favorite shopping area might provide a structure. Each store you pass as you walk down the street could either be a memory peg itself or contain a set of pegs (hardware store, post office, photo processing, fish and chips, etc.). Or the order of your classes during the day (math, science, art, study hall, history, lunch, etc.). Use any sequence of structures that immediately suggests itself to you.

CHECK THIS OUT

Choose Your Memory Pegs

Choose ten additional memory pegs and jot them below.

First structure (e.g., living room) ______________________

11. (peg object, e.g., sofa) ______________________
12. (peg object) ______________________
13. (peg object) ______________________
14. (peg object) ______________________
15. (peg object) ______________________

The structure above suggests structure 2 (e.g., kitchen): ___________

16. (peg object, e.g., stove) ______________________
17. (peg object) ______________________
18. (peg object) ______________________
19. (peg object) ______________________
20. (peg object) ______________________

Repeat the same process you used with your first ten pegs. (See *Practice Your New Trick* on page 7.) If a particular peg doesn't work after several tries, replace it.

Now you have twenty memory pegs. It might be fun to let a friend in on the trick and take turns calling out twenty objects. Don't time yourself or compete at first, unless you find the extra adrenaline helps you to fix the items more securely. And remember: When you use a group of pegs a second time, you erase the first set of images. Once you've mastered this skill—usually in well under an hour—you can take bar bets, challenge coworkers at coffee break, or start cramming for the next exam.

MEMORIZING VERSUS LEARNING

Education is to learning as tour groups are to adventure.[1]

One of the tragedies of "education" is that students are often judged not for what they know but for what they can parrot back to a teacher or on a multiple-choice test form. The theory behind modern education is an admirable one: that it represents a fabulous smorgasbord. If everyone is exposed to at least a taste from every dish at the banquet of current knowledge, he or she will be more likely to eat it later or at least recognize it as edible. In theory this is highly commendable, but in practice it means that sooner or later we run smack into a subject we care nothing about and can't imagine ever needing to know. The teacher exposes us to lots of facts, figures, and opinions. If this is a great teacher, the hated subject suddenly bursts into flames before our eyes, carved by a muse of fire in our psyche, and the entire course of our life is changed forever. If this is an ordinary or less than ordinary teacher, we struggle to stay awake long enough to dump that load of facts back onto a test paper so we can escape forever.

Much of what is being tested is not knowledge or even intelligence. Plainly and simply, most tests test memory. Here are three important maxims for you to remember about memory:

Memory does *not* equal intelligence.
Memory does *not* equal judgment.
Memory does *not* equal knowledge.

The third statement may surprise you, but knowledge is "the sum of what is known." That requires evaluating one piece of information in relation to another. If you can't decide what is probably important or probably true, what is cause and effect or parts of a whole or totally unrelated information, then even an infinite compendium of facts does not represent knowledge. I have two superb examples.

The first is a Russian newspaperman named Shereshevskii. He was written up and studied extensively in the 1920s by a famous Russian neuropsychologist named A. R. Luria.[2] Shereshevskii had total recall. Literally. He could remember hundred-digit numbers and repeat them thirty years later. He could memorize entire books, chemical formulas, and even poetry in languages he didn't know. He could recall a table of four hundred numbers arranged randomly in a twenty-by-twenty grid pattern. His memory wasn't "photographic." He had highly developed *synesthesia,* that is, he encoded incoming information in a variety of sensory ways. For him, numbers and words had vivid colors and smells and sounds.

Before you wish that you were Shereshevskii, you should know some more about his life. He didn't do very well in school. If someone said something to him in two different ways, he recorded it as two separate messages. If someone coughed while he was reading, the cough was recorded along with the words. His entire world was foreground, vibrant and demanding like the colors in a primitive painting, without any shadings or depth. Nothing was more important than anything else. Thus, while he could repeat all of a speech or interview word for word, he couldn't pick out the important points for his news story. Eventually he had to earn his living as a vaudeville act, impressing people with this incredible ability that was actually a curse.

My personal encounter with a Shereshevskii type was similarly poignant. I have always been a great fan of film musicals, so I was ecstatic when I got a list of several hundred early European musicals available on video. Most of the titles were unfamiliar to me. I rushed excitedly to a gentleman who was an acknowledged expert on this subject and asked him if he would do me the tremendous favor of identifying the important films on the list. I suggested a rating system of one, two, or three stars for historical significance and/or entertainment value. I thought this would take him a few minutes at most. He took my list away and I waited expectantly. And waited. When he handed it back to me, it was covered with minuscule writing. He had listed the director, cast, composer, lyricist, and release date for each film—from memory! As I thanked him profusely, I asked again, very politely, if he had any recommendations as to which films I should buy. He looked genuinely puzzled. Although he had seen more than a hundred of these rare films, he hadn't formed any impression of them beyond their vital statistics. Genius and junk were equal to him.

So here's your next maxim.

Intelligence is selective forgetting.

That's right. Bright people remember less than average people because they drop out all the small stuff. They can focus their energy on important things instead of trivia. Before you start patting yourself on the back for losing your car keys again, notice the word "selective." Bright people *choose* what to remember *in* their heads, what to remember *outside* their heads (on paper, in organizing systems, etc.), and what to forget utterly.

SELECTIVE FORGETTING

Conscious selective forgetting is the hallmark of the efficient mind. We are bombarded with billions of bits of information each day. If we tried to log and retain all of them, we'd stop functioning. Fortunately humans are self-centered, selfish creatures who want to know, "Does this affect me?" This built-in survival feature lets us discard most of those billion bits and concentrate on the ones that are relevant, intriguing, self-enhancing, or life-threatening.

The learning process requires lots of deliberate forgetting. Usually we start with predigested input that outlines someone else's perceptions of sequences, categories, cause/effect relationships, structures, and the relevant "facts." This is a good place to start. The danger comes when we limit ourselves, when particular information becomes fixed and we aren't open to replacing it with new data. To stay current, we must consciously discard parts of what we remember. Periodically we have to *forget* what we "know"—how many planets make up our solar system, the name of the world's fastest runner, or the number of human chromosomes. You're familiar with the humorous saying "Don't bother me with facts—my mind's made up"? The parallel would be "Don't bother me with new information—I've already memorized the old."

Most of us hover on the brink of what is popularly called "overload." We feel pressured to do so many things, decide so many things, know so many things, *remember* so many things. Active forgetting helps clear out useless information.

WHAT IS "INFORMATION"?

Information is no substitute for thinking
and thinking is no substitute for information.[3]

Thinking is a process, and information is one of the ingredients used in that process. You might compare thinking to the process of cooking, while information represents the eggs, butter, and flour. (Memory, if you want to continue the culinary analogy, is maintaining a well-stocked pantry.) The result depends on both the skills of the chef and the quality of the ingredients. A superb chef may fail with flawed ingredients, a poor cook can make an unpalatable mess out of the best ingredients.

Information is whatever you *want* or *need* to know so you can function effectively and do the thinking you want to do. The kind of information that is usually responsible for "overload" falls into the *need* to know category, information that offers no immediate pleasure or meaning, but which may aid long-term comfort: financial trends, dental appointments, No Parking after 4 P.M., Closed Mondays. These are the information bits, essential for planning, that clamor for attention and can contribute to overload.

WHAT IS OVERLOAD?

It's not information but *attitudes* that produce the condition we interpret as "overload." Overload is a personal perception. It can only be identified by the results, not by any cause or specific quantity of information being processed. The symptoms include stress, frustration, confusion, depression, guilt, and a sense of being overwhelmed. Overload occurs when the amount and kind of information clamoring for your attention exceeds your desire or capacity to notice.

Samuel Johnson said, "When a man knows he is to be hanged in a fortnight, it concentrates his mind wonderfully."[4] Your desire or capacity to notice can depend on your current mood, your health, your expectations, how much this new information is going to enrich you or affect your life, and the sum of what you already know.

Most information gathering is based on "need to know." But *who* decides what you need to know? Are you riddled with guilt because you don't know the name of the current assistant finance minister of Zimbabwe? Or are you entirely content even though you couldn't find the United States on a map of the world? Somewhere in between those extremes, most of us yearn to be more knowledgeable and informed than we are. But can we really remember everything? Who decides what we are willing to put energy and time into noticing? Who decides what we will let go of so we can focus on something more relevant to us?

"By giving yourself permission not to know," says Richard Saul Wurman, "you can overcome the fear that your ignorance will be discovered. The inquisitiveness essential to learning thrives on transcending this fear."[5]

When you try to pretend that you can remember every name, subject, and event mentioned by others so you won't look "stupid," you are closing yourself to three terrific opportunities:

1. The chance to learn something you didn't know from someone who may have some insights or expertise.
2. The chance to amplify an old memory by giving it new context. ("Aha! I met someone who used to work there.")

3. The chance to make your fellow human beings feel important and good about themselves through sharing their knowledge with you.

I said that overload is a perception, not an actual condition. Very few busy people choose to spend their vacations in a dark, silent room. Usually they go to some exciting new place, sleep less, exercise more, and eat strange food at erratic times—all happily stressful activities. It is not actual stress they seek to remedy but their *perception* that what they are doing is stressful.

This perception can be compared to the fear that most people have when they must speak in public. In my public speaking seminars I show how to experience the natural adrenaline rush on the podium as positive energy for the task, not as a crippling or debilitating fear. Similarly you can meet a surge of information you ought to remember with either of two nearly identical responses:

- Confusion
- Curiosity

Fortunately you can learn to coax yourself or trick yourself or bribe yourself into interpreting your burst of adrenaline as active curiosity instead of confusion and defeat. When you see yourself in charge, energized by your inborn inquisitiveness, and deciding what to notice and what to ignore, "overload" becomes an impossibility.

INFORMATION AND UNDERSTANDING

In Richard Wurman's provocative book *Information Anxiety,* he describes the frustration, guilt, and depression that result from trying to cope with the masses of facts, figures, ideas, and impressions that bombard us from the moment we open our eyes in the morning until we creep into bed at night—and even beyond that. Wurman writes: "The information *transmission* business and the information *storage* business are not the same as the information *understanding* business."[6]

People who are eager to remember more sometimes try to diminish the *amount* of information in their environments. This method offers limited success because as soon as outside stimulation is reduced, most brains go into full-scale production to generate or sort through internal information. (Concentrate on thinking of nothing and see how successful you are.)

The great hailstorm of information pellets that assaults us each day has to pass through several stages before any one of the pellets can be useful to us.

> We have to *notice* it, however reluctantly.
> (Receive the transmission)
> We have to *structure* it so we can understand it.
> (Recognize, compare, combine, evaluate, alter, and perhaps reject the information)
> We have to *restructure* it.
> (Code and file it, so we can retrieve it later)

It isn't necessary to remember every piece of information you encounter. But you can make a tremendous leap toward conquering information overload by learning to recognize and classify each chunk so you know where to go and find it later, if and when you need it. As you pass through the information blitz, you can learn to file information *about* information in your own mental bins, creating your own library index filing system that will let you access an infinite amount of information. Some of these mental sorting structures you already learned in school: counting, the alphabet, basic spatial and scientific knowledge. Some you will invent for yourself or adapt from strategies in this book.

CHECK THIS OUT

THE DIFFERENCE BETWEEN RECALLING AND RECOGNIZING

Recalling a particular piece of information is a lot more work than recognizing it when you run across it. The following questions are based on what you have (or haven't) noticed in this first chapter.

Free Recall: On a separate piece of paper, jot down your impressions and reactions to what you have just read. If you were going to describe this chapter to a friend, what points would you recall? What information is likely to stick? What did you find utterly boring, silly, or useless? Will you forget it or remember it?

Directed Recall: This is usually called "fill in the blanks." Here you are being asked to recall specific bits of information.

1. The "peg" system was developed by ______________________.
2. The memory pegs consisted of ______________________.
3. Some possible uses for memory pegs are ______________________.
4. If you want to fix a concept, not an object to a memory peg, you can do it if you ______________________.
5. To recall a sequence of "pegged" objects years later, you need to ______________________.
6. Richard Saul Wurman said, "Education is to learning as tour groups are to ______________________."
7. Complete the blanks:
   Memory does not equal ______________________.
   Memory does not equal ______________________.
   Memory does not equal ______________________.
8. Complete the blank: Intelligence is selective ______________________.

Now, see if you can *recognize* more answers than you recalled.

1. The "peg" system was developed by (a) Modern memory experts; (b) The ancient Greeks; (c) The Babylonians; (d) The Assyrians.
2. The memory pegs consisted of (a) The rooms in their homes; (b) Their bodies; (c) Carved wooden or ivory pegs; (d) Cue cards.
3. Some possible uses for memory pegs are: (choose as many answers as you wish) (a) Remembering the names of people at parties; (b) As a parlor trick for impressing people at parties; (c) Writing well-

organized letters; (d) Memorizing information for tests; (e) Finding your glasses and car keys; (f) Remembering the key points of your speech or presentation; (g) Memorizing phone numbers.

4. If the thing you want to fix to a memory peg is a concept, not an object, you can do it if you: (a) Alphabetize; (b) Turn the concept into an impression; (c) Turn the concept into a viewpoint; (d) Turn the concept into an object.
5. To recall a sequence of "pegged" objects years later, you need to (a) Repeat it periodically; (b) Write it down; (c) Add new information; (d) Forget it.
6. Richard Saul Wurman said, "Education is to learning as tour groups are to . . .": (a) knowledge; (b) intelligence; (c) curiosity; (d) adventure; (e) judgment.
7. Memory does *not* equal three of the following things: (a) knowledge; (b) intelligence; (c) curiosity; (d) adventure; (e) judgment.
8. Intelligence is selective (a) remembering; (b) forgetting; (c) knowledge; (d) thinking.

ANSWERS

Free Recall: Did you tend to recall an overview of this chapter? Or mostly details? Or both? Have you noticed whether this changes, depending on how interesting or boring you found the original material? (This is valuable information to have about how your unique and idiosyncratic memory works.)

Directed Recall and Recognition: Most people can recognize much more information than they can recall: "Aha! I've seen that before!"

1. The "peg" system was developed by (b) The ancient Greeks.
2. For memory pegs, they used (a) The rooms in their homes.
3. Some possible uses for memory pegs are (b) As a parlor trick for impressing people at parties; (d) Memorizing information for tests; (f) Remembering the key points of your speech or presentation.
4. If the thing you want to fix to a memory peg is a concept, not an object, you can do it if you (d) Turn the concept into an object.

5. To recall a sequence of "pegged" objects years later, you need to (a) Repeat it periodically.
6. Richard Saul Wurman said, "Education is to learning as tour groups are to (d) adventure."
7. Memory does *not* equal (a) knowledge; (b) intelligence; (e) judgment.
8. Intelligence is selective (b) forgetting.

(Most people do significantly better on recognition than recall.)

DAY 2

How Your Memory Works

WHAT YOU'LL LEARN IN THIS CHAPTER

- A dozen important things about how your brain records memories and how you can boost the process

Appreciating your memory is like understanding how your car works. When you know how your mind processes information and what it is and isn't capable of, you can use it more efficiently and are less likely to "strip gears" or "flood the carburetor." Start by recognizing your memory potential. How much you actually remember is determined by

- Heredity—the DNA you got from your ancestors.
- Experiences—how you interpret things and the effect of previous experiences and subsequent experiences.
- Education—how efficient you are at sorting and storing information.
- Desire—how excited you are about what you want to remember.
- Memory blocks—what physical, mechanical, and emotional conditions affect your ability to remember.

In this chapter you may (or may not) choose to remember the following twelve things about your memory. They come in four handy sets of three:

Three *steps* to remembering
- Registration
- Retention
- Retrieval

Three *kinds* of memory
- Verbal
- Visual
- Kinesthetic

Three *stages* of memory
- Immediate
- Short-term
- Long-term

Three kinds of memory *blocks*
- Mechanical blocks
- Emotional blocks
- Physical blocks

That's twelve things. You can remember them or not as you choose. It is a *choice*. There's no reason you should, unless you enjoy patterns and figuring out how things work, and you feel enriched and empowered by this understanding.

Now I'm going to let you in on a memory fact that will probably surprise you. Scan the list above for a few seconds, for as long as it holds your interest. Then put a check next to the items that you are fairly sure you'll remember at the end of this chapter. Put an X next to the items that don't seem to want to stick in your mind.

Here's the news: The chances are overwhelming that your first instinct about what you will and won't remember will turn out to be right. Tests have shown that people are astonishingly accurate at *predicting* what they will and won't recall. Unless you consciously devise strategies for recalling the balky bits, you won't remember them. Your mind already recognizes what it will and won't recall!

This phenomenon occurs because your "mental executive" has already made tens of thousands of decisions about what you should not bother to notice. Many of these omissions are very useful. They keep you from getting bogged down in duplications and irrelevant information. Some of your decisions are emotional. You choose to notice things that make you feel good—or bad, if that is your current mood. *Any* information that reinforces how you want to feel about yourself and the world and that adds to and is reinforced by something you already know will probably stay in your memory bank. And any information that doesn't, won't.

This *doesn't* mean you have to go into psychoanalysis to find out why you forgot Aunt Maisie's birthday or locked yourself out of your car. There are dozens of normal, healthy reasons for forgetting. And it doesn't mean that you can't or won't learn boring or profoundly unpleasant truths—just that the process requires more conscious effort. Fortunately, there are proven strategies for hoodwinking yourself into the state of intense concentration, curiosity, and excitement that ensures memory.

THREE STEPS TO REMEMBERING

Anything you remember for more than a few seconds or minutes must go through the three steps of Registration, Retention, and Retrieval.

Step One: Registration

You get the information. You notice it. A lot of factors can keep you from receiving the information accurately or at all, or you can choose to discard it as irrelevant.

The kind of memory systems taught in most books are intended to help you recall things you *plan* to remember. Such memorizing represents a very small part of the information stored in your brain. The rest is selected from the millions of random bits that fly past you every second—impressions, words, numbers, pictures, smells, sounds, actions, even pressure against various parts of your body from the way you're standing, sitting, or moving. Which of these bits will you bother to notice? Which ones will you recall later when they might prove useful or even essential?

CHECK THIS OUT

What Do You Bother to Notice?

You've just finished a leisurely two-hour stroll on a popular nature path. As you return to the main road, an eager crowd is waiting to ask you questions. (Note: There are no "right" or "wrong" answers. You are just going to observe how you observe.)

1. A police officer shows you a photo of a very ordinary looking man and wants to know if you noticed him among the several dozen people you passed. How certain would you be that you did or didn't see him?

[ ] Absolutely positive I'd remember whether I saw him
[ ] Fairly certain
[ ] Not sure
[ ] Absolutely wouldn't remember either way

Would your certainty level change if it was a woman?
[ ] More certain [ ] Less certain [ ] No change

Would your certainty level change if the person was extremely attractive or unusual looking?
[ ] More certain [ ] Less certain [ ] No change

Would your certainty level change if you were told the person is seven feet tall?
[ ] More certain [ ] Less certain [ ] No change

2. The officer also describes the year, make, and color of a car the man was driving and asks if you noticed it in the parking lot where you parked your own car two hours ago.

[ ] Absolutely positive I'd remember whether it was there
[ ] Fairly certain
[ ] Not sure
[ ] Absolutely wouldn't remember

Would your certainty level change if the car was similar to yours?
[ ] More certain [ ] Less certain [ ] No change

Would your certainty level change if the car was an unusual color or model?
[ ] More certain [ ] Less certain [ ] No change

3. One minute ago, a gray car drove past you. Do you remember the model, year?

[ ] Absolutely positive I'd remember
[ ] Fairly certain
[ ] Not sure
[ ] Absolutely wouldn't remember

The license number?
[ ] Absolutely positive I'd remember
[ ] Fairly certain
[ ] Not sure
[ ] Absolutely wouldn't remember

If the license plate used words instead of numbers?
[ ] Absolutely positive I'd remember
[ ] Fairly certain
[ ] Not sure
[ ] Absolutely wouldn't remember

Would your certainty level change if the car had almost hit you?
[ ] More certain [ ] Less certain [ ] No change

4. A woman holding a dog leash asks if you saw a lost dog on the trail.

[ ] Absolutely positive I'd remember a loose dog
[ ] Fairly certain
[ ] Not sure
[ ] Absolutely wouldn't remember

5. Another woman asks if you saw a seven-year-old boy alone on the trail.

[ ] Absolutely positive I'd remember a child alone
[ ] Fairly certain
[ ] Not sure
[ ] Absolutely wouldn't remember

6. A bird-watcher wants to know if you saw any small brown birds with black striped wings. How certain would you be that you did or didn't see any?

[ ] Absolutely positive I'd remember whether I saw any
[ ] Fairly certain
[ ] Not sure
[ ] Absolutely wouldn't remember either way

Would your certainty level change if you were asked about seeing a bald eagle?
[ ] More certain [ ] Less certain [ ] No change

7. Someone preparing a survey of park use wants you to estimate how many people you passed on the trail.

[ ] Absolutely positive I'd remember accurately
[ ] Fairly certain
[ ] Not sure
[ ] Absolutely wouldn't remember

8. This same survey taker wants you to describe the route you took through the park.

[ ] Absolutely positive I'd remember accurately
[ ] Fairly certain
[ ] Not sure
[ ] Absolutely wouldn't remember

9. The survey taker also wants to know how many signs you passed on the trail and what they said.

[ ] Absolutely positive I'd remember
[ ] Fairly certain
[ ] Not sure
[ ] Absolutely wouldn't remember

10. The police officer is back, wanting to know if you remember the exact time you started your walk.

[ ] Absolutely positive I'd remember accurately
[ ] Fairly certain
[ ] Not sure—depends
[ ] Absolutely wouldn't remember

11. A forest ranger wants to know if you spotted anyone violating the strict no smoking/no campfires ordinance or saw any hazardous conditions that might result in a grass fire.

[ ] Absolutely positive I'd remember
[ ] Fairly certain
[ ] Not sure—depends
[ ] Absolutely wouldn't remember

12. A fashion reporter asks you to describe the latest fashions in hiking wear. Could you list brand-name shoes or clothes by famous de-

signers that you saw on the path? Could you sketch some of the garments you saw? What colors were the most prominent?

[ ] Absolutely positive I'd remember some
[ ] Fairly certain
[ ] Not sure—depends
[ ] Absolutely wouldn't remember

13. What if you were walking the trail, consumed with the euphoria of falling in love, and your newly beloved was at your side? How would this affect what you remembered? If you sang songs to each other or recited poetry, would you be likely to remember other things happening around you?

14. What if you were in deep despair or turmoil and you were walking along, trying to think things through? Would this change what you remembered later?

15. What if you had a terrible cold or had just lost your glasses or your pupils were still dilated following an eye exam? Would this change what you noticed and remembered?

You've just taken a personal survey of the kinds of things that affect what you can recall from random daily happenings. Naturally there's no way to test what you would actually experience on this imaginary stroll, but amazingly your estimation is probably fairly accurate. People notice and recall what they expect to notice and don't notice what they expect not to notice.

That's because we remember the things that interest us, that affect us emotionally (but not *too* emotionally), and that fit in mental structures we've already created. If we have large, pleasurable mental cupboards for information about automobiles, wildflowers, children, dogs, or license plate numbers, we tend to add the new data. If we are distracted or overwhelmed with emotions—positive or negative—we often fail to notice much of what we see. And if input is muddled or contradictory, we tend to record what fits our preconceived patterns and discard the rest: "My mind is made up, don't confuse me with new facts."

Most of the time this is tremendously efficient. It's how you can carry on a conversation in a noisy place or drive on a busy street. You focus on what you want to notice and block out the rest. But occasionally this useful practice keeps you from noticing something important.

There are some whole categories of information that you've already made a conscious decision *not* to notice. Your answers to the questions above will provide some clues and you can probably think of a dozen others. Some of your rejections are culturally dictated, some are situational, and some are highly personal. Unless something happens to make you want to re-evaluate your decision, your noticing mechanisms will ignore this information.

Visualize a sort of imaginary sullen scullion, arms tightly folded on her chest, a cigarette dangling from her lips as she says, "I don't do windows and I don't notice *that*!" It is this mental housekeeper that you're going to have to charm, cajole, and speak firmly to before you can begin noticing new categories of things. Otherwise the information just won't *register*.

Step Two: Retention

You file the information. Again, it is incredibly easy to misunderstand or misfile, making it nearly impossible to find the information again. But in this step you've labeled the carton and sent it off to your mental warehouse.

You've already set up thousands of mental files for information that affects *you*. If something new doesn't relate to anything else you know, you'll probably discard it. It isn't part of a pattern. It seems useless.

It is human nature to form random occurrences and objects into patterns and structures. The simplest way to group things is to notice common features and differences. In a list like

apple	grape
dog	bird

you would probably group apple and grape together as *Fruit* and dog and bird as *Animals*. But if the list also included

airplane	wolf
ivy	car
elm	piano

you could create new headings: *Vines, Trees, Things that fly, Canines, Things needing keys, Methods of transportation*.

Your need to clump together or separate depends on what use you will make of the information. For the purpose of crossing the street, cars, buses, taxis, and trucks can all be considered "cars." Apples, grapes, and some birds could be your supermarket shopping list, while potted elm trees, apple trees, ivy, and grape vines could be plants you'd buy at a nursery.

The opportunities for misfiling information are endless. Do you group "fish" with living creatures or with food? "Orange" with colors or with fruit? "Cup" with bra or saucer? Children tend to sort objects functionally, by how they are used, while adults tend to sort hierarchically, such as "robin" under "bird." Does this mean that it is smarter to group things one way instead of another? (In one intriguing experiment, members of the Kpelle tribe of northern Africa grouped "fish" with "eat" as Western children would do. But when asked to regroup the same list of objects as a stupid person would do, their choices matched Western concepts.[1])

Retention is just as selective as Registration. Imagine that your eye passes over a headline about the latest oil spill. You could dismiss this piece of information outright—not register it—because it seems far away and couldn't possibly affect you. But if you do register and retain it, it will be as an answer to the Big Question: How does this affect *me*?

- Will my favorite TV program be interrupted for news reports?
- Do I know anyone who will be strongly affected by the accident?
- Will it spoil my vacation next summer?
- Will it increase gas prices? Fish prices? Insurance rates?
- Will my business lose or make money because of it?
- How will it affect the rest of the world?

- Will any species become extinct because of it?
- Will laws or regulations be changed?
- Will there be any major political repercussions?
- Will science perfect fusion and end the need for oil?
- If so, what will this do to the balance of world power? To my country? To my business? To *me*?

The questions you ask yourself and the answers that you anticipate will profoundly affect how you structure and store the incoming information. Obviously no two people will respond in exactly the same way to an important event, and therefore no two people will recall identical information.

Labeling is *essential* to structuring.
Labeling is *dangerous* to structuring.

This contradiction is why you *must* be active as you process incoming information, getting most items properly structured the first time, and going back to reevaluate and categorize some things later.

In their book *The Healing Brain,* psychologist Robert Ornstein and physician David Sobel say "... our illusion of a stable outside world is a *consistent illusion that the brain creates*."[2] In other words, we must deliberately distort reality so it makes sense. Otherwise we couldn't sort and store decades of information and then retrieve everything under a particular title at one time.

This distortion and misremembering is both bad and good. It's bad because we often oversimplify dangerously or we deliberately mislabel something so it fits the pattern. It's good because we can use most of our energy to store new information instead of constantly revising and re-indexing our mental card catalogue. Ideally we will be conscious of our mislabeling and re-evaluate the information when we retrieve it: Picasso is a "French" painter, but he was born in Spain; a "flat" road actually follows the earth's curvature.

Organizing Information with Outlines

Whenever you are faced with an overwhelming flood of information, you can collapse and "shut down," or you can perform triage—from the French verb *trier* meaning "to sort"—and act like a paramedic arriving at the scene of a disaster. The skilled medic divides victims into three groups (thus the "tri"): those who are beyond help, those who can be saved with immediate help, and those who can wait for help.

Your informational overload disaster may require more than three groups. Your first retention decision should be whether any information is more important than any other. When I teach business writing, I recommend the addition of a check-off heading for memos that looks like this:

FOR: [ ] action [ ] decision [ ] information

This way writers are forced to decide the purpose of the memo, which keeps them on track, while readers know immediately what is expected of them and can judge where to put it in their To Do piles. Your memory triage list could be similar:

[ ] Very important/main point
[ ] Supports for main point
[ ] Things that seem unrelated to the main point

A classic power tool for organizing and remembering information is the often-maligned *outline*. An accurate outline can sort tangles of conflicting information into a single, simple structure with dazzling efficiency. Sadly, outlines have fallen into disfavor because so few people know how to use them—probably because their teachers didn't either. In my Horror File is one teacher's misguided student handout demonstrating an "outline" that goes like this:

Charlemagne

I. Born 742
  A. Had three wives
  B. Became king at age 26
    1. Kingdom included France, Belgium, Netherlands, Switzerland, Austria, and western Germany
    2. He was six feet tall
II. Had red hair
  A. Led Franks against the Lombards
  B. Ruled most of Europe
  C. Died in 814

Obviously if you were exposed to outlines like that, it's no wonder you find them baffling and unusable. (Some other ways to outline this information appear at the end of this section, under *Answers*.)

If you already know how to outline like a whiz and see the terrible flaws in the above outline, pause briefly to bless your teachers and go on to the next section. If not, try the following organizing exercise.

CHECK THIS OUT

OUTLINING

1. Outlining the Human Body

One of the easiest ways to understand an outline is to use the human body. Here is a list of body parts to be organized.

ankles	eyes
arms	face
bicuspids	feet
chest	fingernails
chin	fingers
elbows	forehead

hair	nose
hands	palms
head	pupils
heels	roots
hips	scalp
knees	shoulders
knuckles	teeth
legs	toes
molars	tongue
mouth	torso
navel	wrists
neck	

Do you immediately see different clusters, groups, and categories of information? If not, start by finding anything that seems to be a part of something else. Fingers are part of a hand. What else is part of a hand? Write *Hand* and then under it, indented, jot anything that is a subcategory. Do any of the items you've chosen seem to be *sub*-subcategories, for example are "knuckles" and "fingernails" subcategories of the subcategory *Fingers*? If so, list them that way, indented further. Go back and cross off all items related to hands from your master list. What's left? Continue organizing the information into

I. Main categories
    A. Subcategories
        1. Sub-subcategories
            a. Sub-sub-subcategories
                (1) Sub-sub-sub-subcategories
                    (a) Sub-sub-sub-sub-subcategories
                        i) Sub-sub-sub-sub-sub-subcategories
                        ii) Sub-sub-sub-sub-sub-subcategories
                    (b) Sub-sub-sub-sub-subcategories
        2. Sub-subcategories
    B. Subcategories
II. Main categories

Your only limitation is that anything divided must have at least two parts. If you have a *I.* you must also have a *II.* If you have an *A,* you must also have a *B.* When you find you have a single fact dangling, you have three choices:

1. Combine it with other information: *Nose and nostrils*
2. Add more information to create subcategories: *Nostrils* and *Bridge of nose* as subcategories of *Nose.*
3. Eliminate it.

Suggest four major headings (groupings/categories) for the human body in top to bottom order:

I. ____________
II. ____________
III. ____________
IV. ____________

Write each of these headings at the top of a sheet of paper and arrange the rest of the information under the main headings in outline form.

2. Outlining Charlemagne

Rewrite the "outline" on Charlemagne that appears on page 37. The teacher has obviously taken miscellaneous information about Charlemagne and scattered it in approximate time sequence over an outline form. But the number of his wives and his age at coronation are *not* information about (subcategories of) the year he was born. Nor are the extent of his kingdom and the year he died subcategories of his red hair. Rearrange this information into a new outline. (Answers are at the end of the chapter.)

Step Three: Retrieval

You recall the specific bit of information or you recognize it when you run across it. You've sent for the memory storage carton. Or you are walking down a memory corridor and there it is: aha! This is what most people call memory.

The warehouse image is convenient but far from accurate. Memory is an activity, not a place. When we remember, we collect information from the electrical sparks of millions of synapses, often making inferences and leaps of insight that weren't encoded with the original input. In one experiment, volunteers were asked to recall specific words. As they tried to remember, the light images of their brains (photographed by painless magnetoencephalography) lit up like Christmas trees, indicating that they were scanning much or all of their brains, not just one spot. The researchers concluded that they were locating, assembling, and confirming the information from a variety of sites.

> *Memory is like a piece of music—it has lots of different parts that come together to create a whole.*[3]

The more synapses that we use to "write" a particular memory, the more ways we have to retrieve it later from the as-yet-undiscovered secret codes of the axons and synapses, the electrical transmitters and receptors in our brains. Remembering a particular thing in several different ways is like putting a collar *and* a harness *and* a leash on a greased pig. We have more chances of grabbing it when we want it. This is why memory strategies often combine visual, verbal, and kinesthetic memory input and retrieval cues. You write it down, read it back, say the name, make a strong mental picture, and maybe even associate it with particular smells, tastes, music, or textures. Once my daughter was studying for a crucial exam. She played a record of a particular piece of music over and over and *over* while she studied until, to this day, I can't hear it without flinching. Then, when she sat down to take the actual test, she turned on a mental tape of the music and got a nearly perfect score.

This wasn't a preplanned strategy on her part, but it worked and has worked for her since. Often sucking on the same flavor of hard candy, smelling the same cologne, hearing the same sounds, and being in the same position in the same type of environment can help you retrace memory paths and retrieve information. That's why people often retrace their steps when they forget what they were about to do or why they walked into a particular room.

Frequency of recall (sometimes called "rehearsing") also contributes to memory. The more often we recall a particular thing, the less brain we need to do it, and the more brain is available to do other things. Many often-repeated memory tasks slide over into habit, requiring conscious effort if we want to *un*learn them. Edward de Bono says:

> *The main purpose of thinking is to abolish thinking. The mind works to make sense out of confusion and uncertainty. . . . to recognize familiar patterns in the outside world. As soon as a pattern is recognized, the mind switches into it and follows along—further thinking is unnecessary.*[4]

Most remembering is recognizing a pattern or a fragment of a pattern and interpreting it as both complete and relevant. If you didn't, you wouldn't be able to walk and chew gum, or read, or know that a cat is a cat no matter which angle you see it from. But to use patterns, you also need to *lie,* that is, to oversimplify deliberately or subconsciously. Thus we group the planet Earth with *Round objects,* although it isn't, and spiders with *Insects,* although they aren't. "These simplicities are useful fictions," says Robert J. Sternberg, "because they enable us to say things concisely, although we know that what we are saying is not quite true."[5]

THREE KINDS OF MEMORY

While we can certainly remember sounds, smells, and tastes, most of our conscious memory is devoted to storing verbal, visual, and kinesthetic information in some combination, using both natural and man-made structures.

One: Verbal

We remember things verbally by giving them labels.

Phone numbers, addresses, lists of presidents and countries fall into this category. Verbal memory—language and numbers—consists entirely of artificial, man-made structures created to label and organize objects and concepts.

Two: Visual

We remember things visually by their color and proportions.

Recognizing faces, the paintings of Renoir, or the color vermilion uses visual memory, usually reinforced by putting verbal labels on the object. (There is some fascinating research showing that people can identify colors for which their language has no names.[6]) Visual memory can be considered "natural" and independent of language, although it can be trained (using language) to a high level of sophistication. Male/female, child/adult, animal/plant, animate/inanimate are some examples of natural structures that can be recognized and experienced without the necessity of language or labeling.

Three: Kinesthetic

This is the spatial recall of your body and the area around it.

Examples of kinesthetic memory are remembering how to type, drive a car, dance, or where the furniture is in your home. Kinesthetic memory is involved in moving yourself and objects and estimating distances and sizes. It allows you to hold up your hands to show how big the fish was that got away.

When you encode a memory verbally, visually, *and* kinesthetically, you have three ways to retrieve it.

THREE STAGES OF MEMORY

For as long as people have been studying memory, there have been conflicting opinions about how it works. Why can't we remember what we had for lunch yesterday when we can clearly recall an event many years in the past? Is memory one system in which information is stored in different intensities? Or is it separate systems, one for what is going on right now and a second one for general "knowledge"—the languages you speak, your culture, your beliefs and experiences?

Current theory is that memory involves three stages, each with different capacities and durations.

One: Immediate memory

Capacity: *thousands—we can notice thousands of snowflakes, pebbles, trees in a forest, people in a crowd.*
Duration: *two seconds or less*

Immediate memory is constantly making comparisons between how things were a moment ago and how they are now. You notice things coming toward you and going away from you. Without immediate memory, you couldn't string words together into sentences or put one foot in front of another to walk down the street. Immediate memory alerts your short-term memory that something may be about to happen.

Two: Short-term memory

Capacity: *seven things*
Duration: *thirty seconds to two days*

Seven seems to be a real biological limitation to human memory. We can force ourselves to visualize seven distinct things but usually no more. After that we must divide the total into smaller units. Even with seven we like to break up the sequence—phone numbers, for example, which are presented as 333-3333. (This apparently inborn limitation has made seven a powerful number in most cultures: Time is often divided into units containing seven days. Legends refer to the Seven Deadly Sins, the Seven Wonders of the World, the seven-year itch, Seven Ages of Man, etc.)

Short-term memory is an active process. It lets us create contexts by linking things together and giving them meanings. It also lets us repeat something just said, even if we weren't really listening: "Of course I heard you, Gwendolyn. You said, 'You don't hear anything I say!' "

A fascinating thing about short-term memory is that it seems to be occasion-specific. You return to the room and recall where you left your notebook an hour ago. You return to the parking lot and recall where you parked the car this morning.

But the occasion-specific aspect of short-term memory offers a fascinating exception to the two-day rule. When you re-experience something you have done in the past—you walk down a street where you haven't been for years or run into someone you rarely see, attend a family Thanksgiving dinner, break your leg—you can be flooded with details about the last time this happened, even though you could not consciously recall them in normal circumstances. You might not recall where you sat during a birthday party two years ago, or who sat next to you, or what you ate, but if you attend a similar party, those details and many more may come rushing back. Were these details actually in your long-term memory? Or is short-term memory accessible longer than we think?

Researcher Alan Baddeley has offered a new model of how we function in short-term memory.[7] He calls it a "working memory," a system that provides temporary storage and work space for complex tasks like language, learning, and reasoning. He theorizes that it consists of three parts: an executive in charge of noticing, a visual-spatial "sketch pad" to manipulate visual images, and a language loop that stores and rehearses speech-based information.

Everyone agrees that short-term memory is the launching pad for arrival in long-term memory. Short-term memory is reading a chapter and explaining what you just read. Long-term memory is retaining the gist of the chapter and even specific details months or years from now. While much "studying" takes place in short-term mode—load and dump, load and dump—the ideal for all that effort is to get some of the information into your permanent library of long-term memory.

Three: Long-term memory

Capacity: *infinite*
Duration: *forever*

Rightly or wrongly, long-term memory is considered the ideal. When some bit of information makes its way to your long-term memory, you can recall it as long as you live, even though this means you carry around a lot of mental trivia.

When you "learn" something, you are attempting to transfer information from your short-term to your long-term memory. Not all of it will stick. If you are bored, learning under duress, and/or convinced that the information is useless to you, you'll be lucky to retain the details long enough to take a test or complete a task. Fortunately, you are able to decide what you want to remember and what you don't. It is a conscious decision. *You* control your memory, and you can move any information into long-term memory by reframing it—using your imagination and ingenuity to make it exciting, bizarre, important, *memorable*.

While short-term memory lapses—misplacing keys, forgetting appointments—are tremendously irritating, long-term memory is what most people are talking about when they say they want to improve their memory. The goal of memory training is to get memory out of the "To Be Filed" pile and into permanent storage in a form that can be retrieved.

Some kinds of long-term memories are never lost, especially visual and kinesthetic. The classic example is riding a bicycle, but you are also unlikely to forget what pineapples or ice skates look like, even if you haven't seen one for years.

Endel Tulving, a Canadian psychologist, theorizes that we have two kinds of long-term memory: *episodic*, which remembers events, and *semantic*, which remembers language and culture.[8] A strong support of this theory is that people with head injuries that impair their memories (*amnesia*) rarely forget the language or languages they previously knew or whether shoes are good to eat.

Getting information into long-term memory can have drawbacks. Occasionally a memory is overwritten so many times that separate events blur into one body of experience. Original perceptions can be colored and changed by subsequent events and suggestions. A study by University of Pittsburgh researchers showed that volunteers could be persuaded to merge an intersection in one location with a stoplight in another, so that they clearly remembered that the intersection had a stoplight. They also looked at a photo of a green car that was constantly referred to as blue. Result: The volunteers started calling it a blue-green car.[9] In another study, young children were told, "You went to the hospital because your finger got caught in a mousetrap. Did this ever happen to you?" All denied it at first, but when questioners repeated the statement over and over at subsequent interviews, the children began to agree and to add elaborate and colorful supporting details of the event.[10] This ability of memory to rewrite itself should make us very cautious and concerned when someone undergoes months of questioning before recalling details of a crime.

No matter how sensible or vigilant you are, your brain will misremember occasionally. This is a built-in feature that allows us to synthesize, to evaluate objects and experiences in general ways, and to recall all we know about a subject, in other words, to *think intelligently*. But obviously misremembering can be inconvenient or dangerous. Be aware of this tricky double-edged aspect of your memory and treat it with great respect.

Most of your short-term memories are soon discarded because you no longer need them. When you decide something is worth "remembering," it still must bypass potential memory blocks before arriving in long-term memory. Once it's there, it is yours forever if you have coded it so you can call it back. You don't have to clean out your memory periodically like an overstuffed closet. Its capacity is limitless.

THREE KINDS OF MEMORY BLOCKS

Everyone gets upset when they can't remember something they want or need to remember. Because memory is such an intimate part of us and our activities, a memory lapse can make us feel dysfunctional, embarrassed, stupid, or like a failure. But there are so many potential and powerful memory blocks lurking in the PAC-MAN maze of memory that it is sometimes a wonder we can remember anything at all.

Mechanical Memory Blocks

You didn't record the information in the first place or you filed it wrong so you can't retrieve it.

Common mechanical blocks include distractions, either when you encountered the information or when you try to recall it, and misinterpreting the information so that it is either discarded or filed in the wrong place, as when you hear the phrase "silver threads among the gold" and file it under *Fashion* instead of *Song lyrics* or *Old age*.

Language offers endless opportunities for mislabeling and misfiling input. Estimating conservatively, at least 30 percent of human communication is misunderstood:

Q: "Do you mind children?"
A: "Yes, I *love* taking care of children."
A: "Yes, I *hate* them. Get the little monsters out of here!"

And consider these double-meaning gems, culled from newspapers:

Police Kill 6 Coyotes After Mauling of Girl
Tuxedos Cut Ridiculously
Shoes Are Required to Eat in the Dining Room
Smoking Ban at Work Helps Employees Quit

English is full of words that have several meanings, even a few with opposite meanings, such as

lease—to rent from or to rent to
enjoin—demand or forbid
stem—start from or stop
cleave—cling together or cut apart

See how easy it is to misunderstand, misfile, and so be unable to recall the information?

There are other mechanical blocks even more ubiquitous. Ringing phones, doorbells, any noise, confusion, or demands for your attention can keep information from registering accurately or at all. But even in the midst of chaos or distraction, a high level of excited curiosity and existing structures can overcome mechanical blocks. For instance, a runner might not notice some odd-looking rocks beside a jogging path, because he or she is focusing totally on the activity, but a jogging geologist or paleontologist could stop dead and go into transports of ecstasy.

One surprising block to memory is concentration. That glorious flow state in which we are utterly focused on the task at hand can produce fabulous results, but it can also keep us from noticing anything else. In August of 1993, Bolivian soccer fans were so engrossed in the televised World Cup qualifying match that they didn't notice their houses were on fire. Forty houses in the village of Ixiamas burned down.[11] And in a charming experiment done at Cornell University volunteers were asked to watch a videotape of a basketball game and press a key whenever the ball changed hands. Afterward, they were asked if they had noticed anything unusual. Very few of the viewers had noticed that an attractive young woman in a skirt had changed places with one of the male basketball players. The intensity of the viewers' task had blocked any information that did not fit in.[12] This is neither "good" nor "bad." Just be aware that intense concentration will block any information that *seems* to be irrelevant at the time.

In another series of studies, people were asked to look at an array of items and remember every item of a particular color. But afterward they were asked questions about other-colored items. Naturally, most could remember what they'd been asked to remember and not what they had mentally discarded. The experimenters concluded: "The strength of memory store is related directly to the strength of attention."[13]

Emotional Memory Blocks

You are trying to protect yourself by not remembering.

Emotional memory blocks exist to protect us. Some people use their "terrible memory" as a powerful tool to shield, comfort, or sabotage themselves. Remembering could have unpleasant consequences, or forgetting provides benefits like extra attention or not having to do something we don't want to do.

Sometimes we hang onto these protective blocks long after we have outgrown their usefulness. Forgetting becomes a habit. Much of my work with people who are blocked is watching them realize that they no longer need this particular form of defense.

We use emotional memory blocks to protect ourselves from perceived harm, error, or ridicule.

Emotional blocks can protect us, but they can also be a dreadful nuisance. When you understand why you have a particular emotional block, then you have conscious choices:

- Dump the block because you don't need it anymore.
- Keep the block because it is still useful and soothing—or even essential.
- Cling to the block for the time being while noticing how it affects your life.

When I polled people in one of my memory workshops about what they wanted to remember or change in the way they remember, a woman I'll call Cecile had an unusual answer.

"I want to remember my trip to China."

"Why?" I asked.

"Because I want to tell my friends."

"Why?"

"Because they always tell each other about their vacations. When I returned from China I thought I'd remember enough to tell them."

"Imagine your friends are gathered here right now," I suggested. "In your mind, see them as you are about to tell them your experiences."

She seemed surprised. "They don't want to hear," she answered.

"How is that?" I asked.

"They'd rather talk about themselves than listen to me," she said. "I'm always the one who listens."

"I'll bet you do have some memories of your trip," I said.

"Yes, but I can't remember the names of any of the places I went."

"Describe one of them," I said.

She began to talk about one city. "That's Xian," said another group member. As Cecile recalled the exciting things she had seen, other people in the workshop supplied the names. Then she realized that even though she couldn't recall the names of the places she had visited (semantic memory) she vividly remembered the places themselves and events of her trip (episodic memory.) She had convinced herself that recalling an experience should effortlessly bring the accompanying data about names, dates, and places. Now Cecile realized that she wanted friends who would share experiences with her instead of playing a frenzied game of "Can you top this?" She left with more understanding and respect for how her mind stores experiences, and with different criteria for choosing close friends.

Not all emotional blocks can be resolved so easily. Some sound simple, but obviously go much deeper. Debbie is a busy and talented art instructor whose "memory problem" puzzled other workshop participants.

"I want to remember phone numbers," Debbie said. "I have numbers that I've called literally five hundred times at work, but I can never remember them."

"Could you write them down?"

"They *are* written down, but I can never find my glasses."

"Could you read them if they were written extra large in a notebook or on a Rolodex?"

"I've thought about putting them in my Rolodex like that," said Debbie, "but I never have the time. I *do* have them written extra large on a sheet of paper, but I keep losing the sheet, so I have to go into the secretary's office and borrow her list and it's very embarrassing—admitting that I need glasses and that I lose things."

"What about taping the list on the wall next to your phone?"

"It's on white paper," said Debbie. "I hate white anywhere in my office."

"Could you write it or photocopy it onto colored paper?"

"Yes. But I only have artwork by my students on the walls of my office."

"Could you get one of your students to make you a beautiful collage, with your color-coordinated large-number phone list as part of the design? You could frame it and no one would suspect what it was."

"Well . . . I'll think about it . . ."

It became obvious that we were playing Eric Berne's game called "Why don't you? Yes, but . . ."[14]

The chances are strong that Debbie *won't* remember phone numbers until something changes in her life. Forgetting them provides some benefit that surpasses any inconvenience or discomfort it causes. Perhaps it is a form of rebellion against higher-ups. Or perhaps Debbie just isn't used to things going smoothly and would feel uncomfortable if they did. (Some people have a high Minimum Daily Self-Harassment Requirement.) Or maybe Debbie uses the drama of losing things as an energizer. Or she may find something rewarding about her daily interaction with the secretary. You can see why therapists love memory blocks. The most bizarre can have simple solutions while the simplest can turn out to be enormously complex.

Physical Memory Blocks

Your entire memory system—that is, your body and your brain—is not physically able to receive or record information accurately.

Physical blocks can be caused by fatigue, tension, illness, pain, poor nutrition, some prescription and recreational drugs, alcohol, nicotine, and lack of exercise. They are much more common and less dramatic than emotional or mechanical blocks.

Even something as "healthful" as a 1200-calorie reducing diet can affect your ability to remember. Healthy volunteers were put on a low-calorie diet in a study by Dr. Russell Wilder of the Mayo Clinic.[15] Within three months they became hostile and nervous, felt persecuted, had nightmares and panic attacks, and lost balance and coordination.

Their attention wandered easily, and they did poorly on tasks requiring *memory*.

Some physical conditions can prevent you from recording certain kinds of information. Being blind, color blind, deaf, tone deaf, or dyslexic will affect what you recognize and how you record it. If you were in severe pain from slamming your hand in a door, you probably wouldn't sit down and try to memorize irregular French verbs. This is common sense—a compelling reason why you should have emergency phone numbers posted next to the phone.

WHAT IT MEANS WHEN YOU FORGET

Has anyone ever chided you with "If it were important, you'd never forget it" or "If you really wanted to remember hard enough, you'd remember"? That's not true.

Memory blocks can mean you *really* want to remember.

Memory blocks don't necessarily mean that you don't want to remember. Sometimes we forget things because we try too hard to remember. We are so anxious to remember that our eagerness gets in the way, like a gamboling puppy about to go for a walk who tangles in the leash and ends up ears over tail.

Will you remember? You tense up. Worry speeds your heart rate, your palms sweat, and your stomach is in knots. The harder you try to recall, the blanker you get, and you are locked into a vicious circle.

There is only one way out. Relax. This, of course, is just what people love to say to you when it is least possible to do so. Nevertheless, your goal is to do what actors do: reframe your sensations and experience the adrenaline rush as energy for the task ahead, not as debilitating terror. When you try and try to remember something and can't, the best way to recall it is to *stop trying*.

CHECK THIS OUT

REVIEW TIME

At the beginning of this chapter, you looked at a list of twelve aspects of memory and predicted which you would probably remember and which you would probably forget. Perhaps something you read was more stimulating (or more boring) than you expected, so your predictions won't be entirely accurate. Let's see. First try to fill in the blanks, a recall exercise.

The three *steps* to remembering are

1. ______________________
2. ______________________
3. ______________________

The three *kinds* of memory are

1. ______________________
2. ______________________
3. ______________________

The three *stages* of memory are

1. ______________________
2. ______________________
3. ______________________

The three kinds of memory *blocks* are

1. ______________________
2. ______________________
3. ______________________

How did you do? Next, see how much of the information you recognize when you see it, a recognition exercise:

The three *steps* to remembering are:

[ ] Rationalization
[ ] Regression
[ ] Registration
[ ] Retention
[ ] Regulation
[ ] Retrieval

The three *kinds* of memory are:
[ ] Visual
[ ] Kinesthetic
[ ] Athletic
[ ] Linguistic
[ ] Numerical
[ ] Verbal

The three *stages* of memory are:
[ ] Short-term
[ ] Long-term
[ ] Full-term
[ ] Recognition
[ ] Immediate
[ ] Retrieval

Three kinds of memory *blocks* are:
[ ] Spelling blocks
[ ] Computer blocks
[ ] Mechanical blocks
[ ] Emotional blocks
[ ] Physical blocks
[ ] Name blocks

ANSWERS

OUTLINING

1. Outlining the Human Body

One way to outline these parts of the human body is

I. Head
    A. Scalp
        1. Roots
        2. Hair
    B. Face
        1. Forehead
        2. Eyes
            a. Pupils
            b. Irises
        3. Nose
        4. Mouth
            a. Tongue
            b. Teeth
                (1) Molars
                (2) Bicuspids
        5. Chin
    C. Neck

II. Torso
    A. Shoulders
    B. Chest
    C. Navel
    D. Hips

III. Arms
    A. Elbows
    B. Wrists

C. Hands
1. Fingers
a. Knuckles
b. Fingernails
2. Palms
III. Legs
A. Knees
B. Ankles
C. Feet
1. Heels
2. Toes

Notice that this body outline is "geographic," top to bottom. If other body parts were on the list—such as blood, muscles, lymph glands, bones, organs, skin—then you would have many more options for dividing up the information and arranging it in an outline, for example:

- From inside to outside
- By function
- In order of formation between conception and birth
- Alphabetically by English or Latin names

2. Outlining Charlemagne

Some ways to outline this information on Charlemagne are:

Charlemagne
I. Key dates
A. Born A.D. 742
B. Became king in A.D. 768 at age 26
C. Died A.D. 814
II. Physical appearance
A. Had red hair
B. Was six feet tall
III. Lifetime accomplishments
A. Ruled most of Europe, his kingdom included France, Belgium, Netherlands, Switzerland, Austria, and western Germany

B. Led Franks against the Lombards
C. Had three wives

or:

Charlemagne

I. Early years, A.D. 742–768
 A. Born A.D. 742
 B. Distinctive appearance
  1. Was six feet tall
  2. Had red hair
 C. Became king in A.D. 768 at age 26
II. Years of his reign, A.D. 768–814
 A. Led Franks against the Lombards
 B. Ruled most of Europe, his kingdom included France, Belgium, Netherlands, Switzerland, Austria, and western Germany
 C. Had three wives
III. Died A.D. 814

REVIEW TIME

Three *steps* to remembering
- Registration
- Retention
- Retrieval

Three *kinds* of memory
- Verbal
- Visual
- Kinesthetic

Three *stages* of memory
- Immediate
- Short-term
- Long-term

Three kinds of memory *blocks*
- Mechanical blocks
- Emotional blocks
- Physical blocks

Go back and compare what you remember with what you *predicted* you would remember at the beginning of this chapter.

DAY 3

How to Master Memory Systems

WHAT YOU'LL LEARN IN THIS CHAPTER

- Ten memory myths
- Your inborn memory structures
- The Link System
- The Rhymed-Number Peg System
- The Shapes-for-Numbers Peg System

If you can read this page, you already possess some powerful basic memory systems. Between going to elementary school and observing the world, you have developed enormous structures for sorting and filing information. These include sorting things

- Alphabetically
- Numerically
- In categories
- In time sequences
- By location
- By opposites
- In series, continuums, and progressions

You also probably know dozens of everyday mnemonic sentences, rhymes, and songs that are an integral part of our cultural folklore:

One, two, button my shoe.
Three, four, shut the door.

or

Red sky at night, sailor's delight.
Red sky at morning, sailors take warning.

or

Thirty days hath September,
April, June, and November . . .

To this repertoire of practical reminders, you can choose to add any of the more elaborate memory systems developed through the ages:

- Peg System (explained in Chapter 1)
- Link System
- Rhymed-Number Peg System
- Shapes-for-Numbers Peg System
- Numbers-Converted-to-Letters System (explained in Chapter 5)

You may find some of these systems tremendously helpful and fun to use—or they may leave you even more confused and frustrated: "If I could remember that 'Banff' means 928 and 'jejeune' means 662, I wouldn't need a memory system!"

Fortunately you are absolutely free to use any or all of these systems, to adapt and personalize them, or to reject them entirely. Consider this chapter a "test drive." You don't have to buy now, just browse and be aware of what's out there on the market.

WHAT DO YOU WANT TO REMEMBER?

When I ask students in my memory workshops this question, they have a wide variety of answers:

"Names. I feel so stupid . . ."
"I want to be able to remember everything I read, not have to study."
"People's birthdays so they won't get angry at me."
"Appointments."
"The important things and not get trapped in trivia."
"Where I put my car keys."
"Our company just switched to a new computer system, and if I don't figure it out soon, I'll lose my job."
"All the ZIP codes in the United States."
"The three-letter symbol for every airport in the world."
"Phone numbers."
"Everything—I'm always overwhelmed!"

As you read this list, you are probably doing three things.

1. You are identifying sympathetically with some of these speakers: "Me too!"
2. You are feeling quite smug because you have already resolved some of these issues in your own life: "Boy, is he dumb! All you have to do is . . ."
3. You are incredulous that *anyone* would expect to remember so much: "Get real!"

The first thing to notice about this list of things that people want to remember is that it refers to at least two kinds of memory: first, to lists that people want to memorize or "learn" (such as ZIP codes, phone numbers, instructions) and second, to things that people want to notice (such as important details, where they left the car keys, names of people to whom they are introduced). It also contains things that could be remembered *outside* the mind, using existing structures such as calendars, notebooks, written lists, or laptops to record phone numbers, appointments and birthdays, shopping lists, even operating instructions for a computer system.

This chapter is going to deal with ways to memorize lists of facts, objects, numbers, or instructions. Why memorize? Why not really "learn" them? It's true that knowing all about American presidents, English kings, or the Table of Elements may be preferable to memorizing a jingle that lets you recite a list. But who decides where your real interests lie and to what you are going to devote time and energy? *You* do. Often "just memorizing" offers immediate returns while providing valuable structures for future learning. It's your choice.

WHY DO YOU WANT RAPID MEMORY?

Most people equate memory with intelligence—or they recognize that other people do. Nearly everyone harbors a secret desire to dazzle the world with amazing insights, infallible decisions, and brilliant solutions to insoluble problems. To do this, they reason, they need to start with an enormous, foolproof memory.

All *healthy* people have a dash of Walter Mitty in their mental makeup. This soupçon of grandiosity is essential for long-term planning, goal setting, and self-improvement. However, when you want to improve just to impress others, it's probably not going to work. What if they still aren't impressed? Are you then even more of a failure? As boring as it is to hear this old saying yet again, there is just no getting away from the truth: *Genuine self-esteem comes from within*. Wanting to appear clever and all-knowing as a way of warding off feelings of emptiness and inadequacy will only increase frustration. Anything memorized to gain the approval of others—even teachers—will soon be forgotten. (Think of cramming for tests. How much did you remember afterward?)

Are there any *good* reasons for wanting to remember more efficiently? Lots. Everyday convenience, safety, pleasure, and self-fulfillment are at the top of the list. The most successful attitude is this: I want to remember better to enrich my understanding, knowledge, and skills because I am curious, eager to learn, and need to know—but I am sometimes willing to take shortcuts to memorize information that seems to be only temporarily useful.

Trying to remember things when you have a poor opinion of your own mental powers is nearly always unproductive. You are much more receptive to new information when you feel powerful, in control, and good about yourself.

TEN MEMORY MYTHS

"Except for torturing rats, probably more psychologists' time has gone into studying memory than any other subject," says psychologist Richard Bandler.[1] All this studying has been useful in demolishing some age-old myths of memory. Here are the ten erroneous ideas most commonly mentioned in my memory workshops, followed by the actual facts.

Myth 1: Somewhere in your brain, you have recorded memories of everything you have ever perceived or experienced.

Fact: Intelligent people learn to block out most of what is happening around them because it is irrelevant to what they are doing and thinking.

Myth 2: Your memories are like photos in an album or statues carved in stone—fixed, permanent, unchanging.

Fact: Memories are constantly being overlaid, eroded, blurred, combined, rewritten, or lost.

Myth 3: Your memories are filed away, each in its own little place in your head, waiting to be retrieved in whole and perfect shape.

Fact: A single memory is coded and stored in numerous parts of your brain, just as a single computer file is stored in various places on a computer disk. When you recall it, you collect all the fragments and fill in the gaps with logic and imagination.

Myth 4: If you are sane, healthy, and truly want to remember, you can recall any information you want on demand.

Fact: Emotional, mental, and physical blocks can keep the healthiest, most motivated person from recalling specific information.

Myth 5: If you can't recall a particular memory, you must be repressing it for neurotic reasons. Unless, of course, you are suffering brain damage.
Fact: Most forgetting is normal, healthy, and useful. Often it happens because the information wasn't presented to you in a way that allowed you to file and retrieve it.

Myth 6: If you can't remember as much as someone else, then there must be something seriously wrong. You should be worried or ashamed.
Fact: Memory capacity is as variable as athletic or music or math ability, and ultimately as irrelevant to success in life. Einstein couldn't remember his own address, General de Gaulle was tone deaf, Mozart had trouble managing money, and Madonna probably couldn't swim the English Channel.

Myth 7: If two or more people have conflicting memories of an event, one of them must be wrong or lying.
Fact: Memory is totally subjective and each person's recollection of an event can be "true" but differ drastically. (Read the history books of several countries about the same war, or recall a family reunion argument about a shared occasion.)

Myth 8: If you recall something clearly, it must be true.
Fact: Studies have proven that memories can be created, erased, or totally distorted, either through natural occurrences or by manipulation of a skilled interrogator.

Myth 9: If you have trouble remembering people's names, phone numbers, or birthdays, that means you don't care about them.
Fact: Often the problem is that you care too *much*. You can make yourself so anxious to remember that your anxiety becomes a memory block.

Myth 10: You will forget more and more as you get older, and senility is inevitable.

Fact: You will remember *differently* as you grow older, but you'll actually have more structures in place to store information. "Senility" can be caused by many temporary medical conditions, including poor diet, depression, and isolation. Alzheimer's Disease, an incurable degenerative condition, afflicts only a minute percentage of older people.

Whatever your present attitude and beliefs about your memory, I am going to tell you something that no other memory book has ever told you.

It's okay to forget anything as long as:

- *You* don't mind.
- *Others* don't mind.
- It's not dangerous.

Guilt is strictly optional. Forgetting happens because you didn't notice the information in the first place or you didn't file it correctly or you were blocked when you tried to retrieve it. Let's start by looking at how your memory uses structures and systems for recording and storing incoming information. Once you understand the process, you can use that knowledge to adapt the strategies in this book or to invent new ones that suit your distinctive needs and temperament.

HOW YOUR MIND WORKS

Your mind has two contradictory desires:

1. It wants to be stimulated.
2. It wants to simplify incoming information.

Structures provide a way to meet both needs. You stimulate yourself by constantly evaluating input and sorting it: "This is the best apple pie I've eaten since I visited my grandmother in Oregon in 1981." Existing structures provide a way to group information into readily retrievable clusters and strings.

SOME COMMON MAN-MADE MEMORY STRUCTURES

Here are thirteen common ways that humans have devised to sort and structure information:

Alphabetically:	a, b, c . . . (in languages that use alphabets)
Numerically:	1, 2, 3 . . . first, second, third . . .
Categories:	animal, vegetable, mineral
	science, literature, mathematics
	mine, yours, ours, hers . . .
Similarities:	four legs: tables and horses
	wet: tears and rain
	roller skates and ice skates
	baseballs and footballs
Opposites:	night and day
	male and female
	young and old
Near each other:	ocean and shore
	road and sidewalk
	picture and wall
Used together:	salt and pepper
	baseball and bat
	soap and water
Part and whole:	toe and foot
	fender and car
	Manhattan and New York
Particular and general:	trout and fish
	gooseberry and fruit
	chair and furniture

Simultaneous events:	pimples and adolescence
	Korean War and President Eisenhower
	night and sleep
Cause and effect:	germs and disease
	fire and heat
	hugs and happy feelings
Time sequences:	happens first, happens second . . .
	1973, 1974, 1975 . . .
	T'ang, Sung, Yuan, Ming dynasties . . .
	caterpillar, cocoon, butterfly
Value sequences:	smallest to largest
	richest to poorest
	least efficient to most efficient

Most of the information in our lives is cross-indexed in two or more of these structures. Think of how you do your income tax forms or sort your laundry or shop at the supermarket.

CHECK THIS OUT

Grouping to Remember

In your everyday life, you frequently organize information by using one or more of the thirteen common structures listed above. Decide which structures and what groupings you could use to help you remember the following sets of things. The order in which you recall them is not important. (There are no "wrong" answers, as long as the structure you choose lets you remember the information. Anything that works for you is right!)

1. eight five four nine one seven six ten three two
2. ceiling rug chandelier floor wall window
3. 77 22 55 11 66 33 99 88
4. lake ocean pond puddle sea
5. banana canary coconut gorilla stop sign airplane bat corn duck
6. apple green lumberjack nurse pine red shoe teacher white

Suggested Solutions

1. Probably numerically: 1, 2, 3, 4, 5, 6, 7, 8, 9, 10
2. A convenient way would be to attach objects to their usual locations and then go top to bottom:
   ceiling—chandelier
   wall—window
   floor—rug
3. All double-digit numbers from one to a hundred except 44
4. Bodies of water in a size progression: puddle, pond, lake, sea, ocean
5. Some potential categories are
   Things that are yellow: banana canary yield sign corn
   Things that are brown and furry: coconut gorilla bat (mammal)
   Things that fly: canary airplane bat (mammal) duck
   Things made out of metal: stop sign airplane bat (aluminum)
   Animals: canary gorilla duck
   Things to eat: banana coconut corn duck
   Things found in the tropics: banana canary coconut gorilla
6. Some possible groupings are
   red apple for the teacher
   green pine for lumberjack
   white shoe for nurse
   or
   apple tree, pine tree, shoe tree
   red, white and green—colors of Italian flag
   nurse, teacher, lumberjack—professions
   ("A lumberjack who hasn't been taught his profession may need a nurse.")

THE LINK SYSTEM

The two most popular memory systems are the Peg System, already described in Chapter 1, and the Link System. In the Link System, you remember a series of things by making vivid mental pictures connecting or *linking* each item to the next on the list. You can link most things to something else in a memorable way if you form a startling image of a powerful connection between them. Harry Lorayne calls this the "Slap in the Face Principle."[2] The connection can be logical or it can be astonishing, shocking, humorous, naughty, absurd—but not so bizarre that you can't recall it. Each item interacts with the next, changing it or being changed by it (piercing, crushing, slashing, enlarging, engulfing, beautifying, lifting, gluing, etc.). Adding imaginary sounds, smells, tastes, and sensations of touch to the connecting images makes them even stronger.

The Link System is very easy to use, and another popular trick for memory demonstrations. The audience calls out lists of utterly unrelated things, such as

watermelon
baby carriage
window
sausages
Abraham Lincoln

I can hear you grumbling that in real life you'd *never* have to remember such a ridiculous list. You're absolutely right. In a minute I'll demonstrate a more practical use for the Link System, but let's use this idiotic collection of things to show how linking works.

Watermelon: A large succulent watermelon (smell it, taste it, stroke its shiny green skin) . . .

Baby carriage: . . . This green watermelon is dressed up in a ruffled pink baby dress and bonnet, lying in a baby carriage. People on the street lean over to look at the cute baby and cry out when they see a watermelon. You tug on the buggy's handlebar, trying to pull the carriage away from them, but the wheels jam. Such a crowd gathers that you and the baby carriage are shoved closer and closer to a huge plate glass . . .

Window: . . . window. The window breaks as the crowd surges forward, pushing you and the carriage through the opening into a butcher's shop. You find yourself standing on broken glass and hundreds of . . .

Sausages: . . . sausages that are everywhere, underfoot, hanging on the walls, and dangling around the neck of the astonished butcher who is . . .

Abraham Lincoln: . . . Honest Abe. He is standing behind the counter in his black stovepipe hat and butcher's apron, looking astonished, sausages looped over his tall hat and lanky shoulders. Just then . . .

And the linking continues for a total of twenty objects. Invariably, once the people in the audience have been shown the technique, they can recite the list in unison. This is all charming nonsense, of course. In daily life, you are unlikely to want to remember any such list! If you did, you'd write it down and save your mental energy for more productive tasks.

What lists *would* you like to remember? One that many people mention is "all the American presidents in order"—as long as it doesn't involve any work, of course. They're not curious enough to actually read about the presidents in depth or study what happened during their terms of office, but not knowing them remains a source of secret, nagging guilt: "I *should* know them."

Linking American Presidents

With forty-one presidents and forty-two presidencies to remember (Grover Cleveland was both the twenty-second and twenty-fourth president), recalling them all in order isn't going to be effortless, no matter what system you use. I've been trying to collect a good mnemonic for presidents for years with little success. There are too many for a really memorable jingle or a logical sentence in which the first letter of each word represents a specific president. A lovely lady named Esther volunteered that she had been taught a sentence in school to help recall the first eleven: *When a just man makes a just vow, he takes pay*. (Hardly a memorable sentence!) "But, Esther," I said, "there are two A's, two J's, two M's, and a P—and is the P for Polk or Pierce? How do you decide what each word stands for?" She wasn't sure either.

Let's try the Link System as a tool for recalling presidents. We start by assuming that most Americans can *recognize* the names of presidents when they hear them, that is when presented with the following list. Check any presidents you recognize on this list below.

Recognizing Presidents

[ ] William Henry Harrison
[ ] George Hamilton
[ ] Abigail Van Buren
[ ] Martin Van Buren
[ ] Richard Benjamin
[ ] Benjamin Harrison
[ ] Benjamin Franklin

(Check your answers against the list of presidents that follows. Unfortunately, some Americans *do* think the illustrious Ben Franklin was a president, but you're not one of them, right?)

To use the Link System, you are going to select a memory image for each president, preferably a distinctive object that can't be confused with something similar. For example, if you are visualizing a piece of furniture, but aren't sure whether to call it a couch, davenport, sofa, or lounge, it won't be much use as a memory trigger.

Your visual images could be symbols, portraying something about the person. For instance, a cherry tree for George Washington and a log cabin for Lincoln—but what would you use for Chester Alan Arthur and Benjamin Harrison?

A simpler method for a list with so many lesser knowns is to suggest the principle *sound* of the name and hope you can fill it in—a moving *van* for Martin Van Buren, a *jack* for Jackson. Here are some suggestions. Choose the ones that appeal to you, that seem most memorable. If none of them suits you, create your own from your personal experiences and jot them in the blank.

CHECK THIS OUT

SOME LINKING WORDS FOR PRESIDENTS

George Washington—So well known that a sound-alike image is probably unnecessary. Think of his image on the quarter, the $1 bill, or in the many official portraits.

Adams—Adam and Eve, ad man, add a man, a dam, Adam Ant, Addams Family, ____________________

Jefferson—(Jefferson appears on the nickel.) Jefferson Airplane/Starship, Jif peanut butter, chef, ____________________

Madison—mad, mad son; Madison, Wisconsin; Madison Avenue, Dolly Madison cakes, Oscar Madison (*The Odd Couple*). He appears on the $5,000 bill. ____________________

Monroe—man row(ing), Marilyn Monroe, ____________________

John Quincy Adams (son of John Adams)—Adam eating a quince in the Garden of Eden, a quick or quivering dam, ____________________

Jackson—an automobile jack, the jack in a deck of cards, jackrabbit, jack-o'-lantern, jack-in-the-box, jackass, jacket, jackknife, jackpot, Michael Jackson, Janet Jackson, the Jackson Five. (Jackson appears on the $20 bill.) ____________________

Van Buren—moving van, Dear Abby (Abigail Van Buren), vanilla bean, ____________________

William Henry Harrison—hair, hairy, hairy son, George Harrison of the Beatles, hare (rabbit), Harrison Ford (star of *Indiana Jones*), ____

Tyler—a tiler (one who lays tiles), ____________________

Polk—to poke, the polka, a polka dot, poker, ____________________

Taylor—tailor, Elizabeth Taylor, tail, ____________________

Fillmore—film, Fillmore East or West (rock emporiums), fill more, film more, ____________________

Pierce—pierce, pier, ____________________

Buchanan—bucket, buckboard, buck (dollar), buckle, ____________________

Lincoln—Old Abe also is so memorable, you won't need a special image for him. He appears on the penny and the $5 bill.

Andrew Johnson—john (toilet), john (pimp), long johns (underwear), ________________

Grant—Grant in his Union uniform, with sword and broad-brimmed hat, is memorable to most. If not, try Grant's Tomb, Cary Grant, an educational grant. He appears on the $50 bill. ________________

Hayes—haze (mist), haze (initiation rite), hay, ________________

Garfield—Garfield the cartoon cat, garden, garlic, garbage, ________________

Arthur—King Arthur, Dudley Moore in the film *Arthur*, Bea Arthur, ________________

Cleveland—Cleveland, Ohio; cleavage, cleaver, Beaver Cleaver. He appears on the $1,000 bill.

Benjamin Harrison (grandson of William Henry Harrison)—all those key words for W. H. Harrison (hair, hairy, hairy son, George Harrison of the Beatles, hare, Harrison Ford) plus something to distinguish him from his grandfather. ________________

Cleveland's second term—a repeat.

McKinley—Mack the Knife, macaroni, Big Mac, Mickey Mouse. He appears on the $500 bill. ________________

Theodore Roosevelt—Teddy Roosevelt, the mustachioed Rough Rider charging up San Juan Hill, may be well known to you. If not, consider his namesake, the teddy bear, or try roses, rows, rowing, roe, rooster, ________________

Taft—taffy, ________________

Wilson—will (document), weeping willow, Mookie Wilson (baseball player), Brian Wilson (Beach Boy). He appears on the $100,000 bill. ________________

Harding—hard hat, hard candy, Andy Hardy, "Kiss me, Hardy," ________________

Coolidge—cooler, coolie, cool ledge, ________________

Hoover—vacuum cleaner, F.B.I. (J. Edgar Hoover), ________________

Franklin Delano Roosevelt (cousin of Teddy Roosevelt)—Another familiar figure for most. If not, try repeats of roses, rows, rowing, roe, rooster, plus something to distinguish him from his cousin Teddy. "Frankly, I'm not Teddy!" He appears on the dime. ________________

Truman—true man, trimmer, trumpet, truant, ________________

Eisenhower—eyes, ice, ice shower. He has appeared on the $1 coin. ________________________________

Kennedy—Well known to most. If not, consider kennel, Ken Doll. He appears on the half-dollar coin. ________________

Lyndon Baines Johnson (no relation to Andrew Johnson)—all those key words for Andrew Johnson (john-toilet, john-pimp, long johns) plus something to distinguish him, ________________. (See your object under a linden tree.)

Nixon—nickel, knickers, Old Nick (devil), St. Nick (Santa), Knicks (basketball team), ________________

Ford—Model T Ford automobile, fjord, ________________

Carter—supermarket cart, brand of underwear, brand of liver pills, brand of ink, ________________

Reagan—ray gun, rags, rayon, ________________

Bush—bush, bushing on motor, ________________

Clinton—DeWitt Clinton (inventor of steamboat), clinker, clinic, Klingon (*Star Trek*), ________________

When you have an image for each president, you link and lock each image to another in a powerful way. Then, as your mind passes over the inevitable sequence, you'll recall each name in order. The more personal you make it, the more easily you'll recall it. Here's a sample of how you might link forty-two presidents together.

Just One Way to Link Presidents

George Washington—You enter an art museum and are astonished to see it is strung with lines of WASHing. By an even more startling coincidence, you find yourself standing in front of Gilbert Stuart's famous portrait of George WASHINGTON, the one that is also on the dollar bill. As you stare at the stern figure, George steps down out of the frame and walks over to a nude marble sculpture of . . .

Adams— . . . ADAM and Eve. They are wearing nothing but fig leaves, and George is scowling. Suddenly his austere face breaks into a mischievous grin. He bends down and peeks under ADAM's fig leaf. Naughty George! But he leaps back, so astonished, that his famed false teeth go flying, for under that fig leaf is—no, not what you were thinking—no, it's . . .

Jefferson— . . . a jar of JIF peanut butter! Imagine Adam unscrewing the lid on this permanently attached jar of JIF and spreading it on a slice of bread! All over the museum sirens go off and neon signs suddenly start flashing: "JIF JIF JIF." George's indiscretion has been taped for one of those hidden-camera commercials by a . . .

Madison— . . . MADISON Avenue Jif pitchman who leaps out with a microphone and rushes at you for your comments. He is dressed like a giant Jif jar, and you know he is from MADISON Avenue because a big street sign is protruding from the top of his head. As bells ring and confetti falls, he thrusts the microphone at you. His head is wagging so hard that the MADISON Avenue sign keeps hitting you on the top of the head. It hurts! How can you escape? You are saved when his attention is distracted by . . .

Monroe— . . . Marilyn MONROE! The Madison Avenue pitchman turns and rushes up to her, shouting, "MONROE! MONROE!" His Madison Avenue sign catches in her blond hair, and she throws up her hands to protect herself, almost dropping a basket she is carrying. The basket is full of quinces. As you gawk . . .

John Quincy Adams— . . . she slinks across the room with her distinctive walk, until she is in front of the statue of Adam and Eve. She begins to feed Adam a QUINCE. His marble lips pucker at the taste. QUINCE juice dribbles down Adam's stone chin and forms a puddle of QUINCE juice at Adam's feet. Marilyn is so enamored of the statue that she begins to cry:

Jackson—"A JACK! Bring me a JACK! I've got to take this statue home with me." Some obliging guards haul in a huge industrial JACK and use it to lift the Quincy Adam statue into . . .

Van Buren— . . . a moving VAN. The jack lifts the statue into the huge VAN, which has rolled right into the art gallery. But the jack mechanism catches on the VAN door and no one can unhook it until . . .

William Henry Harrison— . . . a great HAIRY monster emerges from the cab of the van. The van driver is a HAIRY monster like the one in the Bugs Bunny cartoons. Which HAIRY monster is this? He is wearing a baseball cap with a huge BILL and it says "BILL" on the front of the cap. With brute strength, HAIRY unhooks the jack from the van, leaps behind the wheel, and drives the van right through the wall of the museum, destroying a . . .

Tyler— . . . gorgeous mosaic TILE wall. Tiny bits of priceless TILE explode everywhere. A frantic museum official shouts, "Is anyone here a TILER?" You are covered with huge chunks of broken TILED wall until . . .

Polk— . . . several guards rush over to dig you out. They use the only implements at hand, several POKERS. They POKE at that dusty mound of tile with their POKERS, prying up the huge chunks of tile so you can crawl to safety. But their POKERS also tear huge holes in your tailor-made suit. You are glad to be alive, but POKERS are caught in great gashes in the tailor-made suit. They dangle from the holes, so that you look like a porcupine. You cry out:

Taylor—"TAILOR! What will my TAILOR say? My TAILOR will be heartbroken when he sees what the pokers have done to his beautiful suit!" You are in no condition to be seen in public, so you must rush to your TAILOR immediately for some new clothes. When your TAILOR sees you walk in the door, he immediately . . .

Fillmore— . . . grabs his camera and some FILM. "I must FILM this disaster for your insurance company," he says angrily. The tailor uses roll after roll of FILM until the camera pops open suddenly and his measuring tape entwines around the unspooling FILM. The tailor is so startled that he jumps back, accidentally causing the other rolls of FILM to fly out the window. They sail through the air and land on . . .

Pierce— . . . the PIER below the window. You frantically chase the bouncing film containers as they roll along the rough boards of the PIER. Sometimes the rolls fall through the knotholes in the PIER. You snatch up as much film as you can from the PIER using . . .

Buchanan— . . . a BUCKET. Fortunately the edge of the pier is lined with BUCKETs. Hundreds of BUCKETs cover the pier. BUCKETs hang from pier railings and dangle from the edges. You trip and lose your grip on the BUCKET, which rolls off the pier and lands on . . .

Lincoln— . . . the head of Abraham LINCOLN, who is sitting in a rowboat below. The bucket perches on LINCOLN's head like an oversized stovepipe hat, the kind that he usually wore. Even with a bucket on his head, LINCOLN manages to look dignified. This is even more amazing when you notice that LINCOLN is wearing . . .

Andrew Johnson— . . . bright red long JOHNS! Lincoln is sitting in a rowboat with a bucket on his head, wearing old-fashioned long JOHNS, and still he looks presidential. Suddenly Lincoln begins to writhe about. He is scratching at those long JOHNS. From the trapdoor, cuffs, neck, and between the buttons come crawling . . .

Grant— . . . GRAY ANTS! Huge GRAY ANTS. You've never seen GRAY ANTS before, only black ones, but these are Confederate ants in little gray uniforms! The Confederate GRAY ANTS are crawling all over the long johns, chewing the long johns, biting the long johns, gnashing at those long johns. Their little ant teeth are full of red bits of the long johns. Abe slaps at them with his huge, powerful hands, slapping those GRAY ANTS so hard that they begin to explode, forming a . . .

Hayes— . . . misty gray ant HAZE of ant parts in the air around him. The gray ants are popping like popcorn, vaporized into HAZE by his blows. The HAZE grows and grows. The HAZE is so thick that you can no longer see the gray ants. The whole world disappears in this HAZE. Suddenly from this HAZE emerges . . .

Garfield— . . . GARFIELD, the cartoon cat. He is enormous! GARFIELD floats in the middle of the haze as more haze pours from his nostrils like smoke. GARFIELD is turning into a dragon that's going to eat you. Who can save you from this gargantuan GARFIELD dragon? You need a knight in shining armor!

Arthur—King ARTHUR appears in full armor and attacks the huge Garfield, but Garfield takes King ARTHUR in his giant cat jaws and begins to chew his crown, his breastplate. King ARTHUR is soon covered with Garfield's cat tooth marks and claw marks. Is Garfield going to swallow King ARTHUR?

Cleveland—No! Arthur whips out a giant CLEAVER and hacks his way to freedom. The glittering CLEAVER seems to be an extension of Arthur's chain-mail-clad arm. Arthur is like Edward Scissorhands, except that he is Arthur CLEAVER-hands. Arthur slashes and slashes at his hairy opponent with this mighty CLEAVER until the CLEAVER is . . .

Benjamin Harrison— . . . all covered with bloody cat HAIR. The cleaver is matted with so much HAIR that it can no longer cut anything. (This HAIR is different from the hair of the hairy monster that drove the van. Perhaps Arthur tries to scrape it off into a nearby BIN.) With so much HAIR on his cleaver, the cleaver is rendered useless until . . .

Cleveland's second term— . . . the glittering, razor-sharp edge cuts through the hair, restoring the CLEAVER to its original powerful state. The CLEAVER was made useless by the hair, but now the hair has been conquered by the CLEAVER. The CLEAVER starts to attack the giant cat and finds that instead of sinking into bloody cat flesh, it is now chopping . . .

McKinley— . . . KINDLING. The cleaver is chopping up a pile of thin branches next to a KINDLING pile. Usually an axe is used for this job, but this is special KINDLING that requires the delicate strokes of a cleaver. The freshly cut KINDLING gives off a strong odor because this special KINDLING is from . . .

Theodore Roosevelt— . . . ROSE trees. Someone is trying to make kindling from your gorgeous ROSEbushes and you've caught the villain red-handed. The split kindling reeks of ROSES and you find whole ROSES among the chopped wood. You scoop up the ROSES and have just bent down to smell them when you find . . .

Taft— . . . that hot, gooey TAFFY is pouring all over them. The sticky TAFFY gets up your nose and runs down your arms and legs. You can't pull the roses loose from your hands because they are glued there tight with the runny TAFFY. Fortunately . . .

Wilson— . . . there is a weeping WILLOW tree nearby. You struggle to use the long, wire-like, dangling WILLOW branches like cheese slicers to scrape the taffy off your arms and hands. It works, but then the WILLOW branches are covered with soft taffy. The WILLOW becomes so heavy that it falls over on you. It hits you . . .

Harding— . . . HARD! The HARD trunk of the willow hits you so HARD that your head makes a cartoonlike DING sound. Listen to that HARD DING! Fortunately, you are wearing a sort of HARD hat. Your HARD hat is unusual because it is actually . . .

Coolidge— . . . a picnic COOLER. On your head is a hard-hat picnic COOLER for protection. The hard ding smashes the COOLER into thousands of small plastic pieces. Your head is fine, but your clothes and the carpet under your feet are covered with COOLER fragments. There's nothing to do but . . .

Hoover— . . . HOOVER them up. (Yes, the British use "to HOOVER" for "to vacuum," just as Americans use "to Xerox" for "to photocopy.") Valiantly you HOOVER all those soft, clinging cooler bits until they are totally consumed by the HOOVER. This is a mighty HOOVER, but not mighty enough because . . .

Franklin Delano Roosevelt— . . . your old ROSEbushes that have been lying dormant suddenly spring to life and begin to wrap themselves around the Hoover, like the vines that completely covered Sleeping Beauty's castle. ROSE tendrils circle the bag, the handle, the power cord, clogging the opening at the bottom. The Hoover soon disappears under waving ROSEbush branches, forming a bizarre Hoover-shaped ROSE topiary. It is the stuff of romance novels. If you were writing one, all you'd need now would be a . . .

Truman— . . . TRUE MAN, a storybook hero that rarely exists in real life. But every rose garden must have such a hero, such a TRUE MAN. The TRUE MAN stands in silhouette against the rosebushes, and then turns to spear the heroine with his . . .

Eisenhower— . . . gorgeous, sexy EYES. His EYES make the heroine and the readers swoon. Brown EYES, blue EYES, color doesn't matter, as long as they are piercing, twinkling, and seductive EYES. He is perfect—*too* perfect, for he is really . . .

Kennedy— . . . a KEN DOLL with huge, blue painted eyes. Can you believe that someone actually sits all day painting eyes on KEN DOLLs! Unfortunately, this fictional hero has no more individuality than Barbie's plastic companion, the KEN DOLL. Excuse me, please, but I'm so repelled by this romance novel that I'm going to throw up in the . . .

Lyndon Baines Johnson— . . . JOHN! Shut the JOHN door so you won't hear me! "Urp." You turn on the faucet to mask the sounds of your nausea but . . .

Nixon— . . . NICKELS pour out and make pinging sounds as they bounce around the basin. NICKELS continue to pour out of the faucet until they cover the floor and fill the bathtub. NICKELS everywhere! Your nausea is forgotten as you scoop them up and load them into . . .

Ford— . . . your antique Model T FORD. You are going to use your FORD to get the nickels to the bank. You put bags of nickels in the back seat and front seat and tie them on the running boards of the FORD. But as you are driving your FORD down the road, someone . . .

Carter— . . . pushes a supermarket CART into your path. Your gorgeous restored classic black Ford has a rusty old CART wrapped around its front end. Steam from the Ford engine is rising through the grillwork of the CART, and the CART wheels rest against the Ford windscreen. How can you get rid of this CART? A mechanic arrives with a . . .

Reagan— . . . RAY GUN! Now there is an extraordinary space-age tool that will dissolve the cart. The mechanic turns on the RAY GUN and it's like a science fiction movie. The RAY GUN causes the cart to shimmer and vanish. You go over to inspect this RAY GUN, but suddenly it flies out of the mechanic's hand and lands in a . . .

Bush— . . . BUSH. The ray gun is wedged tightly in the center of a thick BUSH. You and the mechanic both try to retrieve it from the BUSH, stretching out your arms to the ray gun through the dense BUSH foliage. You are both astounded when the BUSH . . .

Clinton— . . . grabs you and holds you tight because it is really a KLINGON, an evil space creature, that has disguised himself as a bush. Its KLINGON tentacles are wrapped tightly around your outstretched arms and you wish you had watched more *Star Trek* episodes so you'd know how to conquer this KLINGON . . . Beam me up, Scotty!

Whew! You've just linked forty-two presidents and two hundred years of history in a few minutes. Quite an accomplishment and not easy, you'll agree. Right now you are probably sitting slack-jawed and glassy-eyed, like the stunned audience of Mel Brooks's satirical musical, *Springtime for Hitler*. Your initial reaction is almost certainly negative. "Ridiculous," is the mildest comment most students make. But a few hours later, when they review the exercise, it is incredible how much they remember, and twenty-four hours later, it's amazing how many find that they can recall most or all the U.S. presidents.

If you find that some of the connective links don't stick in your mind, come up with your own links, using personal images. If you went to Chester Alan Arthur Junior High or live on Buchanan Street, you have some power tools that few others have. Whatever images you choose, you will remember them because you have devoted *time* and *energy* to creating them. They are not imposed by some outside authority. They are your own invention, the children of your imagination, and they will work for you for that very reason.

Let's review the bizarre story you just experienced. If you adapted parts of the tale to your own images, that's great! You'll remember those parts even better.

CHECK THIS OUT

Can You Link the Presidents?

Fill in the blanks below.

	Linking Word	President
The museum is hung with	______________	
and a painting of	______________	1. ______________
who lifts the fig leaf of	______________	2. ______________
and finds	______________	3. ______________
promoted by a pitchman from	______________	4. ______________
who is distracted by	______________	5. ______________
who feeds what to whom?	______________	6. ______________
who is then lifted by a	______________	7. ______________
into a	______________	8. ______________
operated by a	______________	

	Linking Word	President
wearing a cap with a	________	9. ________
who then drives through a	________	10. ________
You are rescued by	________	11. ________
so you need to see your	________	12. ________
who records you on	________	13. ________
that then rolls down the	________	14. ________
and falls in a	________	15. ________
that lands on the head of	________	16. ________
who is wearing	________	17. ________
from which crawl	________	18. ________
that he vaporizes into	________	19. ________
from which emerges	________	20. ________
who is attacked by	________	21. ________
who wields a big	________	22. ________
that becomes covered with bloody	________	23. ________
so he needs another	________	24. ________
that now chops	________	25. ________
that smells like	________	26. ________
soon covered with sticky	________	27. ________

	Linking Word	**President**
that you slice off by using a nearby	____________	28. ____________
which falls on you how?	____________	29. ____________
But your head is protected by a	____________	30. ____________
which shatters and must be cleaned up by a	____________	31. ____________
soon covered with	____________	32. ____________
inspiring a romantic novel whose hero is a	____________	33. ____________
with enormous, sexy	____________	34. ____________
like Barbie's friend	____________	35. ____________
which makes you rush to the	____________	36. ____________
where the faucets gush	____________	37. ____________
that you load in your	____________	38. ____________
which smashes into a	____________	39. ____________
and is removed by a	____________	40. ____________
which flies into a	____________	41. ____________
which turns into a	____________	42. ____________

(*Answers are on pages 84–86.*)

Answers

	Linking Word	President
The museum is hung with	washing	
and a painting of	Washington	1. George Washington
who lifts the fig leaf of	Adam	2. John Adams
and finds	Jif peanut butter	3. Thomas Jefferson
promoted by a pitchman from	Madison Avenue	4. John Madison
who is distracted by	Marilyn Monroe	5. James Monroe
who feeds what to whom?	quinces to Adam	6. John Quincy Adams
who is then lifted by a	jack	7. Andrew Jackson
into a	moving van	8. Martin Van Buren
operated by a	hairy monster	
wearing a cap with a	bill	9. William Henry Harrison
who then drives through a	mosaic tiled wall	10. John Tyler
You are rescued by	poking with pokers	11. James K. Polk
so you need to see your	tailor	12. Zachary Taylor
who records you on	film	13. Millard Fillmore
that then rolls down the	pier	14. Franklin Pierce
and falls in a	bucket	15. James Buchanan

	Linking Word	**President**
that lands on the head of	Abe Lincoln	16. Abraham Lincoln
who is wearing	long johns	17. Andrew Johnson
from which crawl	gray ants	18. Ulysses S. Grant
that he vaporizes into	haze	19. Rutherford B. Hayes
from which emerges	Garfield the cat	20. James Garfield
who is attacked by	King Arthur	21. Chester Alan Arthur
who wields a big	cleaver	22. Grover Cleveland
that becomes covered with bloody	hair	23. Benjamin Harrison
so he needs another	cleaver	24. Grover Cleveland
that now chops	kindling	25. William McKinley
that smells like	roses	26. Theodore Roosevelt
soon covered with sticky	taffy	27. William Howard Taft
that you slice off by using a nearby	weeping willow	28. Woodrow Wilson
which falls on you how?	hard!	29. Warren G. Harding
But your head is protected by a	plastic cooler	30. Calvin Coolidge
which shatters and must be cleaned up by a	Hoover vacuum	31. Herbert Hoover

	Linking Word	President
soon covered with	roses	32. Franklin D. Roosevelt
inspiring a romantic novel whose hero is a	true man	33. Harry S. Truman
with enormous, sexy	eyes	34. Dwight D. Eisenhower
like Barbie's friend	Ken doll	35. John F. Kennedy
which makes you rush to the	john	36. Lyndon Johnson
where the faucets gush	nickels	37. Richard Nixon
that you load in your	Model T Ford	38. Gerald Ford
which smashes into a	supermarket cart	39. Jimmy Carter
and is removed by a	ray gun	40. Ronald Reagan
which flies into a	bush	41. George Bush
which turns into a	Klingon	42. Bill Clinton

THE RHYMED-NUMBER PEG SYSTEM

There are several memory systems that let you attach new things to things you already know, in this case numbers. But since "one" and "eight" don't have distinctive characteristics for most people, the numbers have to be converted to objects. In the Rhymed-Number Peg System, they are converted to objects by using rhymes. You start by noticing common rhymes for numbers from one to ten:

one	bun, sun, gun, nun
two	shoe, glue, stew
three	tree, key, bee, sea, flea
four	door, floor, whore

five	hive, drive
six	sticks, bricks, chicks, ticks
seven	heaven
eight	skate, gate, crate, date, plate, slate
nine	vine, pine, wine, spine, stein
ten	pen, hen, wren

Naturally you can use *any* rhyme that comes into your head since no number under ten rhymes with another. Then to remember up to ten new things in order, you simply attach them to a number rhyme. For example:

Number: one
Thing to Remember: George Washington
Rhyme: sun
Combining Image: lines of WASHING that are drying in the sun

Number: two
Thing to Remember: John Adams
Rhyme: shoe
Combining Image: naked ADAM wearing nothing but a fig leaf and huge army shoes

Number: three
Thing to Remember: Thomas Jefferson
Rhyme: key
Combining Image: spooning JIF peanut butter from a jar, using a huge key

Number: four
Thing to Remember: John Madison
Rhyme: floor
Combining Image: Messy Oscar MADISON of *The Odd Couple* is leaving his clothes all over the floor.

Number: five
Thing to Remember: James Monroe

Rhyme: hive
Combining Image: A MAN ROWS a rowboat with a huge beehive in it, as the bees circle around his oars, buzzing.

Number: six
Thing to Remember: John Quincy Adams
Rhyme: bricks
Combining Image: Naked ADAM is smashing QUINCES with bricks.

Number: seven
Thing to Remember: Andrew Jackson
Rhyme: heaven
Combining Image: Michael JACKSON, in a beaded angel costume, is being hoisted up to heaven.

Number: eight
Thing to Remember: Martin Van Buren
Rhyme: skate
Combining Image: a VAN full of roller skates

Number: nine
Thing to Remember: William Henry Harrison
Rhyme: vine
Combining Image: HARRISON Ford as Indiana Jones is swinging on a vine.

Number: ten
Thing to Remember: John Tyler
Rhyme: hen
Combining Image: A hen is pecking at the ground, eating small squares of yellow TILE instead of corn.

If your mind doesn't run to rhyming, you may prefer a counting system that uses shapes.

THE SHAPES-FOR-NUMBERS PEG SYSTEM

Another memory system that lets you attach new things to things you already know is the Shapes-for-Numbers Peg System. This works best for strongly visual people.

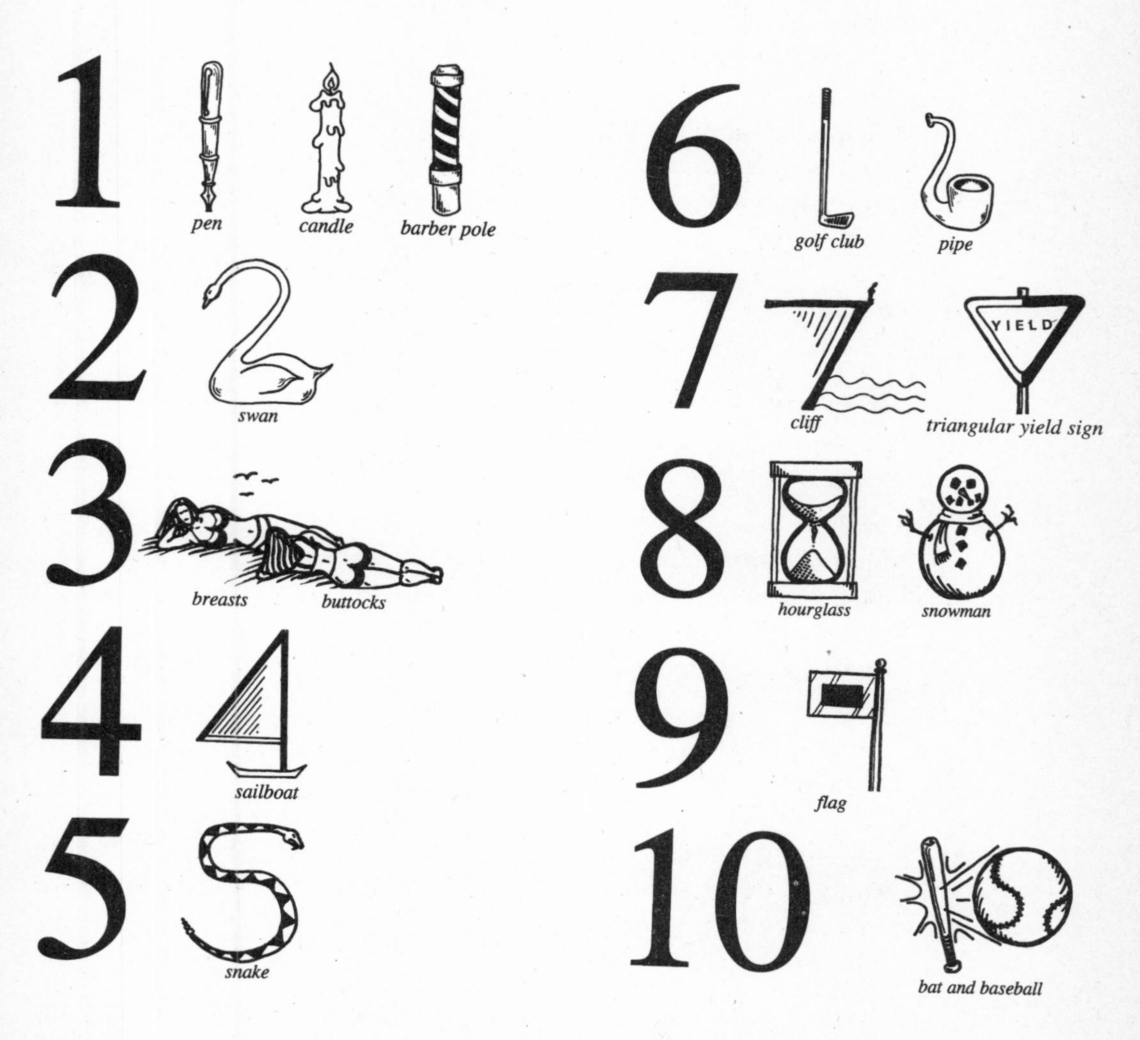

Again, you can use *any* image shaped like a number, but it helps to limit yourself to one set of images. Otherwise it is too easy to turn a pipe upside down to form either a six or a nine. When you have selected your look-like-numbers object pegs, you attach new information to them with a strong interacting image. For example, let's say that you want to remember ten presidents, and to vary the images, let's also say that your list of ten begins with President James Polk:

Number: one
Thing to Remember: James Polk
Visual Number: pen
Combining Image: A pen is POKING an ink-stained hole in your shirt pocket.

Number: two
Thing to Remember: Zachary Taylor
Visual Number: swan
Combining Image: A TAILOR is trying to sew little coats for swans (Grimm Brothers fairy tale).

Number: three
Thing to Remember: Millard Fillmore
Visual Number: buxom bathing beauty
Combining Image: buxom bathing beauty wound round and round with a shiny strip of movie FILM

Number: four
Thing to Remember: Franklin Pierce
Visual Number: sailboat
Combining Image: A sailboat is PIERCED by a bolt of lightning that leaves a huge, gaping hole. Or a sailboat is tied up to a PIER.

Number: five
Thing to Remember: James Buchanan
Visual Number: snake
Combining Image: a huge BUCKET of wiggly snakes

Number: six
Thing to Remember: Abraham Lincoln
Visual Number: golf club
Combining Image: Lincoln is playing golf on the golf LINKS.

Number: seven
Thing to Remember: Andrew Johnson
Visual Number: cliff
Combining Image: Contestants are tossing dozens of porcelain toilets (JOHNS) off a steep cliff.

Number: eight
Thing to Remember: Ulysses S. Grant
Visual Number: snowman
Combining Image: A snowman is made of GRANITE.

Number: nine
Thing to Remember: Rutherford B. Hayes
Visual Number: flag
Combining Image: Francis Scott Key is trying to see the Stars and Stripes, but it is obscured by HAZE.

Number: ten
Thing to Remember: James A. Garfield
Visual Number: bat and baseball
Combining Image: GARFIELD the cartoon cat is wearing a baseball cap, his ears sticking out on each side, and he is playing baseball.

A PREVIEW OF ONE MORE SYSTEM

You've now had a taste of four of the basic memory systems to choose from. There is one more number system which will be explained in Chapter 5, *How to Remember Dates and Numbers*, but you can preview it here. It is called the Numbers-Converted-to-Letters System. With this technique, you take a long hard-to-recall number and convert the individual numbers into consonants. Then you try to form words and sentences by adding vowels, spaces, and periods. For example:

	3	2	9	3	0	5	2	3	0	8
converts to:	M	N	P	M	S	L	N	M	S	F

and, with a bit of imagination, you create a memorable sentence using these letters, such as "Many poems line my safe"—or readily forgettable nonsense like "Men pay muslin. I name sofa."

Don't worry if this doesn't appeal to you. There are lots of other ways to remember numbers. You can even write them down.

IT'S OKAY NOT TO LOVE SYSTEMS

Systems are like diets. Some work great for some people and not at all for others. If you still haven't found an organizing technique that appeals to you and that you'll find playful and fun to use, that's okay. Stay relaxed and open-minded, confident that when you *need* to know something and *want* to know it, then you can usually find a way to remember it.

Any reasonable memory-organizing system works
if you enjoy using it.

No memory system, however flawless,
will work if you don't enjoy using it.

When you need and want to remember, you'll figure out a way. It may be an elaborate centuries-old system, or it may be a mischievous lyric to your favorite song. Both are equally effective.

CHECK THIS OUT

Test Drive a System

Start by deciding on something that you *genuinely* need and want to recall—some list that would give you pleasure whenever you recalled it from memory. Then choose any of the systems discussed in this chapter that you found appealing. Play matchmaker. See if your list and the system are a good combination. If not, wait awhile and try another. Stay curious, be open to new techniques, and, above all, have fun.

Developing Your "Incidental" Memory

Up until now we've been dealing with information that you want or intend to remember. Virtually all scientific memory testing concerns things that people actively try to remember. But what about all the minutiae that drifts past each day without your noticing it? Some of it pops back later as delightful trivia, but most is lost because you never bothered to notice. However, sometimes this background information can prove very useful later. Fortunately you *can* train yourself to notice more.

Here's an entertaining classroom training exercise that you can use at home to expand your "incidental" memory.

Get a pencil and paper or tape recorder. Shut your eyes and describe the room where you are sitting in detail. How many windows, how many chairs, how many shelves on the bookcase? Are the numbers on the clock Roman or Arabic? Who else is in the room? Exactly what are they wearing? Who is wearing earrings? Loafers? If you are alone in a very familiar room, go back to the last time you glanced out the window or down the hall. Exactly what did you see? Or choose a nearby place you have visited often. Write or talk your description. Then check it out the next time you go there.

The people who do well on this exercise are usually the ones who played friendly observation games with their parents when they were young. Mommy or Daddy would ask, "What's that? Can you name it?" or "Where have you seen something like that before?" Being able to recall brought praise and pleasure.

You can now play this game with yourself anytime, anywhere. Look away during a lecture and try to summon up the design on the tie of the speaker. Then glance back and check out your answer. Soon you'll rival Sherlock Holmes in your ability to recall details.

DAY 4

How to Remember Names

WHAT YOU'LL LEARN IN THIS CHAPTER

- What it means when you forget names
- Active strategies for recording and recalling names
- Survival techniques for those awkward moments when you forget a name

"All white men are named Bob," says comedienne Marsha Warfield, "and all Black men are named Tyrone."[1] Wouldn't that make life simple? W. C. Fields encountered a similar memory-Utopia in his film *Million Dollar Legs*,[2] when he was informed that all the men in the mythical kingdom of Klopstokia were named George and all the women Angela.

"Why?" he asks.

"Why not?" the heroine (Angela) replies.

Forgetting people's names is the second most common memory complaint, surpassed only by "Where did I *put* it?" Not recalling names can be annoying, embarrassing, costly, rude, bad for business, socially devastating, physically dangerous, and occasionally disastrous to our love lives. People assume we are being snooty or stupid or uncaring. Nearly everyone wants to remember names more efficiently, but despite powerful internal and external motivations to do so, nearly everyone doesn't. It is a universal paradox that the harder we try to remember, the less likely we are to succeed.

Fortunately, it's rarely our fault. Society has seen to it that we simply are not going to remember names. Only with the cleverest strategies can we dodge the memory traps laid for us. Here are some of those responsible for our predicament.

Blame Your Parents

If you have a hard time putting names to faces, you can blame your parents. (You may already blame them for everything else, so one more thing shouldn't bother them.) As a small child you responded lustily to every new face that came along. You shrieked with terror or stared with wonder or howled with glee. If anyone had a distinctive characteristic—a huge nose, a foolish hat, a missing limb—you gaped. When you heard a new name, you responded delightedly with a rhyming if unflattering mnemonic: "Icky Dicky," "Fatty Patty potty-face," "Mrs. Brewer smells like a sewer."

In an effort to civilize you, the adults in your life were constantly tugging on your arm, whispering, "Ssst! Hush! Don't stare. Don't notice." Most of us are still following this noble directive. In modern society, there are a great many things that polite, politically correct, compassionate people are not supposed to admit they notice about the people they meet. But by not observing, by not labeling, you lose most of the handles that let you file and retrieve information later.

Blame Other People's Parents

Of the seventeen girls in my grade school class, five were named Carol, four were named Nancy, three Barbara, and three Janet. That left Priscilla and me. To this day I confuse the four names, calling a Carol Janet or a Barbara Nancy. There were also five Bobs and three Johns. My son has no such problem. His classmates include: Raven, Angel, Fabrice, Taffeta, Song, Dariouche, Abidine, Aisling, and Mederic.

So you see that you can readily blame other people's parents for (a) giving their children common names, and (b) giving their children uncommon names. Of course, the commonness of names is highly subjective. I once worked with an Israeli who spoke flawless Oxford English but who was completely unfamiliar with Anglo names. It was an odd and enlightening experience. He found Bill and Steve as exotic and hard to remember as I found Yerhehmiel and Na'ama.

Blame Kitchen Appliances

Until fifty years ago, few would dare to throw even a modest party unless they had servants or could hire some for the event. The servants prepared and served the food while the host and hostess "worked the room," introducing each newcomer to another guest or two, pointing out an area of mutual interest, and shepherding the first few minutes of conversation. As soon as this cluster of strangers had established rapport and committed each other to memory, the guest was gently moved on to another group.

Then along came freezers, dishwashers, food processors, and microwave ovens. Whether it was cause and effect or the advances of democracy, live-in servants vanished from most homes. Today the hostess (and sometimes the host) arrives home from work and disappears into the kitchen. When you ring the doorbell, she appears, flushed and wiping pâté from her fingers, to greet you, then turns to the assembled crowd: "Everybody, I'd like you to meet Jack. Jack, this is Tom, Cindy, Roger, Teddy, Paul Elder and Paul Edelman, Mel and Stacy, Marcia and her son Peter, and, let's see, oh, that's Sandy and Jackie in the corner over there. Make yourself at home!" And she's gone.

That's not an introduction. That's a modern form of torture!

Blame the Extraordinary

We all marvel at the feats of the glorious few who can greet thousands of people by name although they may not have seen them for years. We read about the extraordinary name-recalling abilities of Napoleon, politician James Farley, and businessman Charles Schwab. On television we see memory experts demonstrate their skill by calling out the names of everyone in a sizable audience. These people share three qualities:

1. They have an inborn ability.
2. They have powerful motivation.
3. They use both to perfect a skill.

These remarkable people are held up to us as role models. "You could do the same thing if you really wanted to," we are told. Some of us believe this. Do we then feel better and more confident because of this belief? Do *you*? Or do you still feel a bit helpless and inferior because you haven't straightened out the two Paul's at that party and aren't sure which was Cindy and which was Sandy?

Fill in the blank: Believing that I can perform like someone so extraordinary that they make the record books is ______________________.

We all need realistic goals. Our memory capacity may be limitless, but our time and energy aren't. If being able to greet everyone by name is the most important thing for you, you will devote the necessary personal resources to it and you will do it. Some of us have other ways to spend our life's assets.

WHOM DO YOU REMEMBER?

A study of face recognition by the very elderly found that they recognized many more famous faces from their younger days—that is, from the 1930s and 1940s—than from the 1980s.[3] While the researchers didn't philosophize about this result, it is easy to imagine why it occurred: We remember people we are connected to and identify with during the happiest, busiest times of our lives, even if we never meet them. That's why some people go to reunions and some don't. Fellow survivors of a shared experience stay strong and vibrant in our memory all our lives. If it was a positive connection, we enjoy re-experiencing it. If not, we don't.

When people between fifteen and seventy tell you, "I can never remember faces" (or names), they may be trying to make you feel good by demonstrating a presumably shared shortcoming. Actually they are warning you that they are not going to remember you. How do you feel? If they are telling the truth—if they actually have no memory of names or faces—then you are allowed to feel genuinely sorry for them. They may have prosopagnosia, a rare neurological condition that prevents people from recognizing faces. Their life must be hell. But few of us, no matter how often we blank on names or walk past an acquaintance on the street, forget *all* names and faces.

CHECK THIS OUT

What Sorts of People Do You Remember?

Yes, yes, you're terrible at remembering people. Let's find out *which* people you don't remember. Check the appropriate boxes below. (Ignore categories that aren't relevant.)

I can recognize and name at least fifteen people in the following categories:

[ ] family members and relatives
[ ] friends
[ ] acquaintances
[ ] coworkers in my department
[ ] workers in other parts of my company
[ ] company officials
[ ] janitors and cleaning personnel
[ ] customers
[ ] teachers

[ ] students in my classes
[ ] fellow students not in my classes
[ ] church or club members
[ ] television celebrities
[ ] film stars
[ ] baseball players
[ ] political office holders
[ ] cashiers, salespeople, news vendors, garage attendants, and other service personnel whose services I use
[ ] painters
[ ] composers
[ ] musicians
[ ] chess players
[ ] fashion models
[ ] wrestlers
[ ] world leaders

Add any other categories in which you can recognize and name at least fifteen people:

[ ] ______________________________

[ ] ______________________________

[ ] ______________________________

Do you see any pattern? Can you remember people close to you, but not celebrities? Or vice versa? (Remembering people you've never met better than people you have may mean you are trying to protect yourself from uncomfortable personal relationships.) You probably have no trouble remembering lots of people in an area that interests you, whether it's basketball or ballet. Are you better at remembering "higher-ups"? Or "lower-downs"? If so, what could explain this? What patterns have you established for noticing and not noticing people?

If you checked at least two categories, you are not memory-impaired and should be able to expand your people collection. You've heard of baseball cards? Imagine that you are collecting mental shoe boxes of "people cards," photo and name on the front, vital statistics on the back.

Treasure the rare and odd ones, while taking pleasure in your ever-expanding archive.

INTRODUCTIONS

Someone is walking toward you, hand outstretched. You take his hand as he tells you his name. What is going through your mind?

Hand warm. Grip medium. Nice gray shirt. What is that cologne? About an inch taller than I am. Glasses—are those bifocals? Is that smile genuine? Is that a toupee? How does his company affect my company? How important is he? He might not like me. Do I like him? (Slight adrenaline rush, sweaty palms.) Everyone's looking at me. Did someone just ask me a question? Is my fly open? What the heck was his name?

How *Not* to Remember People When You're Introduced

- Concentrate on what they may be thinking about you.
- Concentrate on what you should or shouldn't say to them.
- Concentrate on worrying about whether you'll remember their names.

How to Remember People When You're Introduced

- Decide to remember.
- Be impressed before you hear the name.
- Listen to the name.
- Repeat the name.
- Lock the name to the face.
- Ask if you don't hear it clearly or can't recall it.

Decide to Remember

Someone in this crowded room is your long-lost uncle who wants to give you a million dollars. If I whisper his name in your ear, will you forget it?

Be Impressed . . . Before You Hear the Name

Usually you have a few seconds to size up the person before you hear the name. If I were teaching juggling, I'd say, "Throw before you catch!" With names, see before you hear. Frequently, we don't hear names because we are busy taking in what impresses us visually. It's as if we can't see and hear at the same time.

Focus on a feature. Look as you did when you were that curious, gaping child: "Oooh! What big ears!" or "I've never seen such gray eyes!" Later on you can easily adjust and refine your first impression.

Sometimes the person has no immediately noticeable characteristics. None. He or she is a total blank to you—gray, mousy, nearly invisible. Pretend this is a disguise and make up a colorful alter ego: "Obviously a strip-o-gram dancer" or "champion mud wrestler." You have only three seconds to do this, so make it simple. Imagine him in a gold-lamé jockstrap, twirling his discarded leather chaps over his head. Imagine her in a bikini, coated with mud.

Listen to the Name

This is the moment that most memory books go into high gear. You are offered hundreds of sound-alike images for the names you will hear: "mini-injure" for Minninger, "do gain" for Dugan. If this is how your mind works, you probably do this already and don't need massive charts. If this is *not* how your mind works, you'd again be in the position of having to remember two new things instead of one.

For most of us, the easiest way to remember something new is to attach it to something—or some*one*—we already know. Ask yourself:

- Does the person look like the name? If not, why not?
- Do I already know someone with this name? How do they compare? How alike? How different?
- The same name as a celebrity? Compare them or imagine them interacting.
- A literary or historical figure?
- An occupation? (Baker, Barker, Chandler, Miller, Forester, Cooper,

Smith, Mason, Marshall) How would this person look dressed for this job, with the tools of the profession in her hands?

- An object? (Bentley, Finn, Rose, Kerr, Ford, Gable, Byrd, Post, Chin, Angelo) Picture the person in, on, or with the object.
- A bird? (Robin, Jay)
- A jewel? (Ruby, Opal, Pearl)
- A flower? (Rose, Iris, Daisy)
- A month? (April, May, June)
- A brand name? (Campbell, Dolby, Thomas, Kraft, Welch, Yamaha, Hershey, Levi) Imagine the person using the product or with his photo on the jar or box.
- A major company? (Macy's, McDonald's, Sears, Borden) See the person as a balloon in the Macy's parade, or holding a Big Mac or a Sears catalog, or hugging Elsie the Cow.
- Something in nature? (Hill, Dale, Vallee, Rhoades, Forest, Brooks) This person is wading in a brook, standing in the middle of a busy road.
- A place? (Plymouth, Cleveland, Kerry, London) Visualize the person in the setting, leaping off onto Plymouth Rock or straddling the Thames like London Bridge.
- Can you rhyme it? (Hairy Mary; Not-Slim Jim; Pickle-Nose Nichol; Blake, Blake, eyes like lakes; Russell, Russell, muscle man) Don't worry if the rhyme is rude or naughty, as long as it is accurate and memorable. No one but you will know about it.
- Does it truly sound like a familiar word or phrase? (Ask you for Askew; have a land for Havilland) Can you connect this phrase to the person in a logical way?
- Can you add a euphonious descriptive word to the name? (Frowning Fred, Joking Jackie, Sloppy Sloan, Bosomy Bowman)
- Are the first and last names both usually used as first names? (Tony Bill) Or last names? (Taylor Caldwell)
- Does the last name end in "son"? If so, can you use the first part of the name to imagine that the person is shrinking into a smaller version, a "son" of it?
- Is the person a woman whose last name ends in "son"? Masterson, Johnson? Mentally change it to Masterdaughter or Johndaughter. In amusing yourself, you will make the name more memorable.

- Can you translate the name into English from another language? (Black for Schwartz, high mountain for Altamont, green for Verdi, thread maker for Tessier)

Any connection you make between a person's name and another image must be intensely personal. No one else's gimmick or mnemonic is going to work for you. You'll never remember it in the pressure of an introduction or when trying to recall it later, and you don't need it. You already possess an absolutely enormous personalized catalog of people and things to relate new people to.

Repeat the Name

Is it Huffman or Hoffman? Mark or Mike? Take your time and focus. Try to ask a question.

"Katherine? I bet there are more different spellings for Katherine than any other name. How do *you* spell it?"

"Fischer? With a c? Are you related to Sam Fischer at Capitol Computers?"

"Hi, Ed. Do you prefer Ed or Edward? Or is it Edwin, like my cousin?"

"Betty, you're Brenda's sister from Portland? Your parents certainly liked names starting with B's—but Betty must be short for Elizabeth, yes? Like Queen Elizabeth, except probably no one calls *her* Betty."

As you shake hands, say your own name. This gives people both an auditory and kinesthetic impression of you. Shaking hands was originally intended to show your hands were free of weapons, but it remains popular because it is the perfect way to slow down and concentrate on new names.

Lock the Name to the Face

Here's where you use those images you created when you first heard the name and saw the face.

Her name is Jill? See her tumbling down a hill holding a pail of water. Or think of "Jolly Jill." Or "Nurse Jill gives me a pill." Is his name Dan? See him in Biblical robes surrounded by lions in the lions' den. Or he may be singing "Danny Boy" in kelly-green knee breeches while holding a shillelagh. Or he's wearing a coonskin cap as Daniel Boone.

Here are just some examples of how you might personalize new acquaintances:

Phil Reid—Phil—fill, teeth not too good, I bet he has lots of fillings, reed, thin like a reed, does he read a lot, looks bookish with those horn-rim glasses. His thinning hair sure *doesn't* look like the luxuriant locks of Phil Donahue.

Shawn Dubin—Shawn is an unusual name for a woman; she's a dancer and I can see her twirling a huge silk shawl, as flamboyant as her personality, its iridescent fringes matching her eye shadow—Ted Shawn of the Dennis-Shawn dancers of the 1920s; Dubin, don't know anyone named Dubin, but I know a Dugan, and the b of Dubin upside down becomes the g of Dugan—spin the central letter.

Renee Donoff—She pronounces it "ree-nee," like the British pronunciation of Irene—"I-ree-nee" in *The Forsyte Saga,* but this Renee is brunette, not blond, and she doesn't look tragic at all; Donoff, down off? How do you get down off an elephant? You don't, you get down off a duck? She laughs a lot, must have a good sense of humor. Imagine her riding on an elephant's back, carrying a duck. Sitting behind her is Nyree Dawn Porter, who played Irene in the Galsworthy TV saga. Both are laughing.

Joe Savage—not at all savage, very tame, but I'll imagine him in leopard skin, his cute little pot belly hanging over the leopard skin, and his hair standing up in spikes. I've never known a Joe, but my very proper Aunt Jo would have been astonished to see this Joe in his savage costume. I can just see her face.

Personalize, personalize, personalize. You may know lots of Jo's, but probably none could be as memorable as my own dear Aunt Jo is to me.

Ask If You Don't Hear It Clearly or Can't Recall It

Although you've done everything right, you'll still find that you can't recall some names. Don't worry. It's a great compliment when someone you met a short while ago turns to you, looks at you as if you were very important, and says, "Tell me your name again."

CHECK THIS OUT

Don't Remember This Person

When you are introduced, plan *not* to remember the person. Stay passive and notice your mental processes as you *don't* focus on the name. (You are probably being distracted by other things happening in the room, by sensations in your body, and by the self-talk going on in your mind.)

PICTURE THIS

A custom once frowned on but now more and more popular is to have your photo on your business card if you have a lot of contact with others. These cards can be great memory joggers, helping you remember others and helping them remember you.

When I taught at the University of San Francisco, I wanted to greet my students by name, but each new year brought 150 new faces. When they were in their assigned seats, I could look at a diagram of the classroom, but what about when I met them elsewhere? I resorted to taking their photos and making flash cards. I'd go through the stack in odd moments, and when I was confident about a name, I'd set that card aside. Finally there would be only a few students' names that I could not seem to remember. I'd confuse two students or go completely blank.

Happily a therapist friend, Arthur Rissman, helped me realize what these few students had in common: They were usually among my favorites! I traced the problem back to a time in my childhood when people I liked kept leaving. Very cleverly I had decided not to remember people I liked, so it wouldn't hurt so much when they were gone. As an adult I could re-evaluate this habit because I now had the power to see people again if I wanted to.

This story illustrates three points.

1. Forgetting names can mean that you *care*.
2. We can decide to change memory habits that are no longer useful.
3. Making photo flash cards to learn large groups of names is a practical and effective technique.

Forgetting names can mean you *care*.

WHY DO YOU WANT TO REMEMBER NAMES?

A highly touted benefit of remembering names is "success." This appeals to both our highest and lowest motives. On the plus side, we make others feel good about themselves when we remember them. On the negative side, it may indicate we feel a need to control others: "If only I could do that," we reason, "I'd have real power over people." You bet!

If you are terrific at remembering names, you'd make a good salesman, politician, union organizer, or public relations person. You could also qualify for a career as a greeter in a hotel or restaurant, or as the aide who stands at the elbow of royalty and presidents, whispering the name of the next person in the reception line. You can probably think of a few more job categories in which expert name-recallers can shine. You could even go on TV as a memory expert. Yes, you'd do well in all these professions—if you are *also* smart, hardworking, honest, well-groomed, educated, even-tempered, ambitious, charismatic, self-effacing, courteous, congenial, and/or caring. An ability to summon up names is a very useful skill, but not a substitute for genuine interest and compassion.

CHECK THIS OUT

Name Games

Practice remembering names. You can use people from a real situation in your life in which you'd like to know more names. Maybe you have a stack of business cards with photos on them. Or you can cut photos out of a newspaper or magazine. The business section announcements of promotions and the social section with its wedding announcements are good sources for full-face portraits with captions underneath, but any photos will do.

Collect about fifty newspaper photos—or as many as are in the real group you want to remember. Study each name and face for five seconds or so while deciding on a strategy for recalling the name and attaching it to the face. When you've done all the photos, start over, this time covering the name.

When you're confident about a name, put that photo to one side. Shuffle the photos occasionally like a deck of cards. When a particular person gives you trouble, try to figure out why your strategy didn't work and formulate a new one.

You don't have to complete this project at one sitting. Come back to it over a period of time. As with learning to read and tying your shoes, practice makes perfect.

"YOU CRAZY AMERICANS"

The morning after I'd done a presentation at a Mexican resort on How to Remember Names, I was chatting with a pleasant Italian gentleman named Pipo. He said he hadn't attended, had no interest in how to remember names. I was surprised and asked why. "You Americans are too crazy," he explained. "You want to remember names before you find out if the person is worth remembering. That's not natural. We Europeans make contact first to see if we want to remember you."

WHAT TO DO TILL THE NAME COMES

Busy people have to collect graceful ways to solve the "whatzisname?" syndrome. One outspoken doctor I knew who had trained thousands of students would greet familiar-but-nameless faces with a jovial "So, who the hell are you anyway?"

His wife, less flamboyant, preferred "I remember you so well, but your name has slipped my mind!" In this way, she celebrated her recognition of people. It was the names, not them, that she had forgotten. Saying, "Your name has slipped my mind," is so much more graceful than an apology. You are saying, in effect, "I am human and I care."

You can use either his or her line (I recommend the latter) or try any of these first aid lines until the name comes. Each has its drawbacks.

"How are things going?"

Useful response: "Great. We just got the Widget account and I've been made regional sales manager. We sure miss you."

Useless response: "Great."

"How long has it been?"

Useful response: "Let's see, must have been at the class reunion two years ago."

Useless response: "You asked me that question two weeks ago."

Embarrassing but useful response: "You asked me that question two weeks ago at the Chicago conference."

"How is everyone?"

Useful response: "Okay. Martha's thinking of leaving sales and going back to nursing. And Tony's in the middle of finals."

Useless response: "Okay."

"What are *you* doing here?"

Useful response: I just flew in from Topeka to finalize the sale of our house. I don't know what you and Bill are going to do if you decide to sell—property values in the neighborhood have sure dropped since the freeway went in. And, of course, I wanted to see all the old gang at Wonder Widgets while I'm here."

Useless response: "The usual."

Embarrassing but useful response: "I live here. Across the street from you—for the past three years."

"What have you been doing since the last time I saw you?"

Useful response: Your mother's probably told you already—our bowling club is going on to the County Bowling championship next month.

Useless response: "Same old thing."

As an absolutely last-ditch survival technique, a man I know named Paul carries around blank Rolodex cards in his pocket. When he has chatted for a while with someone he obviously should know and still hasn't a clue, he whips out a card and a pen, saying, "I'm *so* glad I ran into you because my Rolodex accidentally got thrown out when I moved to a new office. I'd be grateful if you could write down your current address and phone number for me." So far, no one has refused. Later, on the back of the card, he jots down when and where he met the person plus a brief description.

THE ULTIMATE STRATEGY

Give yourself permission to blank on names occasionally. Otherwise you're playing "Let's pretend that I can remember everyone I've ever encountered." Tension, guilt, and self-harassment are optional and utterly useless. Be kind to yourself. Cheerful curiosity and an unflappable sense of humor can get you through any "whatzisname?" situation.

DAY 5

How to Remember Dates and Numbers

WHAT YOU'LL LEARN IN THIS CHAPTER

- How to use numbers you know to recall new numbers
- The Numbers-Converted-to-Letters System
- The Counting-Equivalent System
- The Phone-y Number System
- How to measure and expand your digit span

Shereshevskii, the Russian memory whiz, experienced numbers as colors, shapes, sounds, and personalities. For him the number one was a "proud, well built man. Two was a frolicsome woman, whitish in color, flatish and rectangular.

> *. . . 3 a gloomy person (why, I don't know); 6 a man with a swollen foot; 7 a man with a moustache; 8 a very stout woman—a sack within a sack. As for the number 87, what I see is a fat woman and a man twirling his moustache.*[1]

Because Shereshevskii found numbers as memorable and interesting as people, he could envision them interacting with one another, and so he easily remembered long strings of digits. To keep them in sequence, he would position his number-people along streets he knew, standing in doorways, peeking out of windows, leaning against fences and lampposts. For him, a lengthy number was as full of drama and as richly plotted as a novel or a film.

Even if seeing a number doesn't flood your mind with emotions, colors, textures, and meanings, you find significance in more numbers than you realize. Read this story and see how much you understand:

> The moment 99 said, "Give me five," 007 knew his bachelor days were numbered. Soon 2 were made 1, but they were incompatible from the start. She brought her cassettes of *1776* and 9 on the honeymoon, but all he wanted to listen to was 2 singles. That first night they quarreled so loudly over whether to watch the 49ers or *8½* on TV, that the neighbors nearly called 911. Sulking, 99 retreated to the bedroom with *1984,* while 007 stormed off to the nearest 7-11, where he bought some 409 to clean his 32. Driving back, he pulled into a 76. 99 was a perfect 10, he reflected as he waited in line, and a boon to his 1040, but maybe it was time to say 10-4 . . .

Translation: The moment Control Agent 99 (Barbara Feldon on *Get Smart*) shook hands with James Bond, his bachelor days were numbered. Soon they were married, but they were incompatible from the start. She brought her cassettes of two Broadway shows on the honeymoon, but all he wanted to listen to was his Metallica and U2 singles. That first night they quarreled so loudly over whether to watch football or a Fellini movie on TV, that the neighbors nearly called the police. Sulking, she retreated to the bedroom with a George Orwell novel, while Bond stormed off to the nearest convenience store, where he bought some all-purpose cleaner for his gun. Driving back, he pulled into a gas station. She was very desirable, he reflected, and an income tax deduction, but maybe it was time to say good-bye . . .

See how much personality numbers can have? Numbers, like words, can be emotional as well as informational because, like words, they are artificial, man-made structures. Both are abstract symbols and sounds that represent a concept.

FORGET WHAT DOESN'T WORK

Many of the techniques and systems for remembering numbers that are described in this chapter may strike you as harder to remember than the numbers themselves. If so, forget them for now and just chant the number over and over until it is locked in your memory. Anything that works for you is great. The point of showing you so many techniques is to provide you with a smorgasbord of systems to choose from. Pick whatever works for *you* and ignore the rest.

STRATEGIES FOR NUMBERS

Remembering numbers and dates works the same way as remembering words, with the advantage of one added strategy. The first two number/date strategies are similar to those you already use for remembering language:

1. Relate new numbers to ones you already know.
2. Make the numbers so exciting, so intriguing that it is impossible for you to forget them.

Your third bonus strategy is:

3. Convert numbers to letters and words.

Of course, many number sequences suggest their own strategies. There's 1-2-3 and 2-4-6-8 and the more sophisticated Fibonacci sequence—1-1-2-3-5-8-13-21-34—in which each new number is the sum of the previous two numbers. Fascinatingly, the Russian mnemonist Shereshevskii was oblivious to the value of numbers. When presented with the following grid:

1 2 3 4
2 3 4 5
3 4 5 6
4 5 6 7

he didn't recognize the simple progression and set about his intensive placing of the numbers down a street.[2]

WHAT'S THE EASIEST WAY?

The easiest way to remember most numbers, dates, times, bank balances, and statistics is to *write them down*. Remember outside your head. Knowing how to retrieve information is usually just as effective as knowing the information itself.

Sometimes, though, it's better to be able to remember them. Teachers insist that students recall numbers for exams. Salesmen need to rattle off style numbers and prices if they want to appear knowledgeable and function efficiently. Librarians must know the Dewey Decimal System. Police need to remember statute and code numbers when citing lawbreakers. Scientists and pilots, supermarket cashiers, carpenters, and truck drivers all need to recall numerical information—there are few occupations that don't involve remembering *some* numbers. And all of us can save lots of time, expense, and aggravation in an emergency if we can recall rarely used numbers like family social security numbers, insurance policy numbers, bank account numbers, certain PINs, combinations, or car registration numbers. Of course we have these numbers written down in what we hope is a safe place, but recalling them on the spot could be enormously useful, maybe even a lifesaver.

So the "easiest way," writing numbers down, may not be good enough for every situation. Let's consider three strategies for recalling numbers.

STRATEGY 1: RELATE THE NEW TO THE OLD

Where were you when the Challenger blew up? Where did you live when you were in third grade? Most people date recent events by using their own lives as a calendar. Few people can't tell you where they were and what was happening in their lives when historical events occurred that strongly affected them: Pearl Harbor, the first human on the moon, the deaths of President Kennedy, Malcolm X, Robert Kennedy, Martin Luther King, Jr., Marilyn Monroe, or John Lennon. People who have moved around a lot date events by where they were living at the time. Some go by which job they held, who they were married to, or which child was on the way or had just arrived. We use these memories as interlocking cues for establishing when something happened.

The calendar provides other annual signposts—Christmas, Independence Day, Bastille Day, Cinco de Mayo, Guy Fawkes Day, birthdays, and anniversaries. Most of us recall some key dates from history class and popular literature: 1066, 1492, 1776, 1812, 1914, 1929, 1941, 1984, 2001. We also have long lists of numbers that we've memorized over the years—addresses and telephone numbers, locker numbers, padlock combinations, radio station positions on the dial, even pi (π), the Greek letter symbolizing the ratio of the circumference of a circle to its diameter, which is 3.14 to math novices, 3.141592+ to the more advanced.

Numbers can also be imprinted in our memories from non-scholarly sources. When I took my young son to see the movie *Amadeus,* and Tom Hulce as Mozart was looking poorly, my son leaned over and whispered, "Is it December fifth?"

"I have no idea. Why?"

"Well, if it is, he's going to die." I was astonished. Afterward I asked him how he had known.

"Because that's what it says on 'Rock Me, Amadeus'—Falco's hit single."

Some people who can remember numbers easily do so by relating them to numbers they already know. In an interview with *Washington Post* reporter T. R. Reid in 1989, psychology student Rajan Mahadevan refused Reid's business card and committed the telephone number to memory: ". . . only 10 digits [and it contains] the series 623, which is reminding me of Avogadro's number—you know, the atomic weight constant." Mahadevan made the *Guinness Book of World Records* memorizing pi to the 31,811th digit. "The 31,812th digit . . . ," he added, "I'm always stumbling over that one." His favorite portion of pi was the hundred numbers between 2,901 and 3,000: "I don't know why I love those digits so much. It's like seeing a woman and you just like her from the first for no reason."

Mahadevan doesn't have eidetic (photographic) memory. He rates only high average at remembering verbal information and is worse than average at recalling faces. He was the subject of a National Institutes of Health study by scientists trying to figure out whether memory is a single network or separate abilities.[3] (Considering the number of people who can remember some kinds of things superbly and others poorly, this would seem to be a foregone conclusion, but scientists are a "Show me" lot.)

Pi is popular among number mavens, partly because it is infinite and rarely repeats any sequence of digits, and partly because, like Mount Everest, it is there. In 1993 a Minnesota man, Michael Harty, wrote out 7,777 digits of pi from memory, missing only fourteen of them. It took him nearly two hours. Unlike Mahadevan, who sees the numbers as distinctive entities, Harty converts them to alphabet equivalents and then makes up words: "Line 1 is a picture of a bow tie, and it's tearing, that is, it's crying, on a tulip, which moves away and picks up a device, which puts a big notch into a yellow mule. The yellow mule becomes quite upset, and he grabs a big box of a laundry detergent called Fab . . ." Harty, thirty-nine, said he plans to memorize pi to 1 million digits.[4]

Consider the following common phrases and concepts associated with numbers. You probably can add many more. These familiar signposts can serve as raw materials for making images of more complex numbers. You may enjoy linking numbers to images in creative ways, combining familiar numbers and numerical concepts as a tool for remembering longer numbers.

1—1-track mind, 1-night stand, 1-way street, 1 wheel on a unicycle

2—2 wheels on a bicycle, 2 hands, 2 feet

3—3 Musketeers, 3-ring circus, 3 R's, 3 meals a day, 3 blind mice, 3 wheels on a tricycle

4—4 seasons, 4 legs on a dog or table, 4 Horsemen of the Apocalypse

5—5 fingers on a hand, a nickel, 5 and dime (variety store), 5 on a basketball team, give me 5, a 5th of whiskey

6—6 feet under, 6th sense

7—7 days in the week, 7 dwarves, 7 Deadly Sins, 7th heaven

8—8-ball, 8th wonder of the world, dinner at 8

9—9 lives of a cat, 9 pins, 9 on a baseball team, cloud 9, 9 months pregnant

10—10 fingers, 10 little Indians, 10 Commandments

11—11 people on a football team, the 11th hour (last minute), 11's (British coffee break)

12—12 months in a year, 12 in a dozen, 12 Apostles, 12-mile limit, 12th Night

13—Friday the 13th, a baker's dozen

14—2 weeks, a fortnight

15—15 men on a dead man's chest, 15 minutes in a quarter hour

16—Sweet 16, legal driving age in most states, "You're 16, you're beautiful . . ." (classic rock-and-roll song)

17—teen fashion magazine, Heaven 17 (disco group)

18—voting age, 18 holes on a golf course

19—19th hole (golf course clubhouse)

20—20 questions, 20th century, "Then come kiss me, sweet and 20" (Shakespeare)

21—legally an adult, a New York restaurant, blackjack card game

22—22-caliber gun

23—23 skidoo

24—24 hours in a day, 4 and 20 blackbirds baked in a pie

25—25 cents in a quarter

28—28 days in February (usually)

29—29 days in February in leap year, year of the last stockmarket crash

30—30 days hath September . . . , Judas' 30 pieces of silver, *thirtysomething* (TV show)

31—31 days in January, March, May, July, August, October, December

32—demisemiquaver (1/32 note)

39—Jack Benny's age

40—40 days and nights of rain on Noah's ark, 40 carats, 40 winks, Ali Baba and the 40 thieves

42—42nd Street (Times Square)

45—"Only 45 minutes from Broadway" (George M. Cohan song)

47—Black 47 (Irish folk-rock group)

48—48 hours (2 days, and also the name of a TV news show and an Eddie Murphy film)

49—49ers (California gold rush), 49ers (football team)

50—50 million Frenchmen, 50–50, golden anniversary

52—52 weeks in the year

55—55 m.p.h. (common speed limit), "I can't drive 55" (Sammy Hagar song)

60—60 seconds in a minute, 60 minutes in an hour, *60 Minutes* (TV news show)

64—64-thousand-dollar question, hemidemisemiquaver (1/64 note)

66—Route 66

69—sex manual illustration

76—Spirit of '76, "76 Trombones" (Meredith Willson song)

77—77 *Sunset Strip* (old TV series)

87—"4 score and 7 years ago . . ." (Lincoln)

90—90-day wonder (quickly commissioned officer), 90-pound weakling

99—99 bottles of beer on the wall, "90 and 9 sheep which went astray" (Matthew 18:13)

100—a century, pennies in a dollar

365—365 days in the year

400—the 400 (exclusive New York social set)

500—the Fortune 500 (stocks)

600—"Into the mouth of hell rode the 600" (Tennyson)

90210—Beverly Hills ZIP code and name of TV show

You can combine familiar numbers and numerical concepts (counting, adding, dividing, etc.) to create your own mnemonics for unfamiliar numbers. Here are some examples:

351—address of Empire State Building (350 Fifth Avenue) plus 1; or a progression of odd numbers: 3-5-7—but the last number has lost its roof and so is demoted to a 1

492—1492 without the first digit

628—double the first three digits of pi (314)

2713—40 minus 27 equals 13; or my favorite age (27) and least favorite age, the first year of being a teenager (13); area code for Los Angeles (213) with a lucky 7 inserted

4002—double 2001 (title of Stanley Kubrick's 1968 film)

5681—year of Lincoln's assassination (1865) backward

6889—7000 minus 111 equals 6889; or a series of four 8's (8888) but the first and last 8 have lost part of their top and bottom loops respectively

9291—Lawrence Welk's countdown for blastoff ('n' 2 'n' 1); or 1929 backward

77639412121400—776 is the date of the Declaration of Independence with the first 1 dropped off; 39 and 41 are the numbers on either side of 40; 212 is the area code for New York City; 1400 Pennsylvania Avenue is the address of the White House. Your connecting fable: After signing the Declaration of Independence when I was forty, I left New York to become President and live in the White House."

CHECK THIS OUT

ASSOCIATING NUMBERS

Write down five useful numbers that you'd like to know. Then devise a strategy for remembering them, using general knowledge, math, and/or personal data that you already know very well.

Your Numbers	Your Strategies
1. ________	________ ________
2. ________	________ ________
3. ________	________ ________
4. ________	________ ________
5. ________	________ ________

Review (*rehearse*) your recall strategies when you finish this chapter and again when you finish this book. You'll surprise yourself at how well you recall the numbers.

STRATEGY 2: MAKE THE NUMBERS EXCITING

You remember how Rajan Mahadevan found numbers emotionally stimulating: "It's like seeing a woman and you just like her from the first for no reason." Most of us *can* get excited about numbers when they represent something to us: a winning score for our favorite team; the amount of a raise or inheritance; the size of something we want lots of or want none of; profit or loss; the difference in miles, dollars, pounds, inches between where we are and where we want to be. But few of us can imagine being aroused by numbers that are entirely abstract and separate from meaning.

This is where the least mathematically inclined can shine, because they often have strong verbal abilities. If you have an overwhelming need to remember a long number and you possess a vivid imagination, you can weave a number into an enchanting and unforgettable tale.

Usually it's easiest to recall a long number if it is divided into clusters, for example:

3 4 3 1 7 8 1 1 3 2 5 9 9 8 1 1 2 6 9

could become:

3 4 3 - 1 7 8 - 1 1 3 2 - 5 9 9 8 - 1 1 - 2 6 9

and you'd find a memory cue for each chunk. But with a story technique, you'd use your imagination to weave the numbers into a continuous story, for example:

> 3 bears sat down to breakfast at a 4-legged table and started to eat from 3 bowls. The porridge didn't suit them so they went for a walk, exiting through the 1 door and down 7 steps through a gate with a big brass latch

shaped like an 8. As they strolled along the road, they met 1 man on 1 horse that had only 3 legs, so between the 2 of them they had 5 legs. This man was carrying 9 chickens and each chicken was laying 9 eggs, which made 81 eggs. The man divided the eggs up into separate sets of 12, which gave him 6 dozen, but he had 9 eggs left over . . .

And you could continue as long as your storytelling ability held out. The effort you put into creating this memory structure contributes as much as the structure itself to your ability to recall the number later.

Shorter numbers can become riveting and charged with emotion if you pretend they represent something of value to you: "I've lost 4.189 pounds this week!" "Interest on my bonds just went up 3.022 percent!" "Wow! Madonna just gave me her unlisted number—064-8239!" Let the child in you make the numbers impressive, irresistible, enchanting.

STRATEGY 3: THE NUMBERS-CONVERTED-TO-LETTERS SYSTEM

If you love crossword puzzles, you may enjoy learning a system that converts numbers into letters. A conversion system should be your last resort because it can be hard work. Try this strategy only if:

- You see numbers as incomprehensible, boring, perhaps even slightly menacing, and you absolutely can't remember them.
- Your verbal memory is strong, and you get pleasure from solving word puzzles.

Unless your word skills are much superior to your number skills, replacing one thing with another will only be confusing. Some memory books have huge charts of word equivalents for numbers. If your eyes cross and your knees grow weak when you see one of these, don't give up. What I'm going to show you is a way to create your own user-friendly conversion system that lets you change numbers into letters of the alphabet. My personal system is somewhat different, and quite a bit simpler than most. If the reasoning behind my choice of letter-number combinations evades you, you are free to make up your own. This is a technique, not a mandate.

In the Numbers-Converted-to-Letters System, each number from zero to nine is assigned a consonant. You transcribe each number into a letter, just as you did with comic-book spy codes as a child. Here are the consonants that I use:

1 = T (one vertical bar)
2 = N (two vertical bars)
3 = M (three vertical bars)
4 = R (its last letter)
5 = L (the 5 fingers of your left hand, thumb extended, form an L)
6 = B (6 and lowercase b look alike)
7 = K (lucKy 7)
8 = D (a script D has two loops)
9 = P (a P backward looks like 9)
0 = Z / S (zero or spent/exhausted)

So the individual numbers from 0 to 9 would be translated like this:

0	1	2	3	4	5	6	7	8	9
Z/S	T	N	M	R	L	B	K	D	P

Once you have mastered these switches, you have two options. You can insert "free" vowels wherever you wish to form words. Or you can use the letters as the first letters of a series of words in a hopefully memorable phrase.

Examples

Phone numbers	5 8 3 - 2 9 4 8	LeaD MaiN PaRaDe
	L D M N P R D	Lie, DaMN PRuDe
		Let's Dance, My Naughty, Pretty Rita Darling
	3 8 6 - 1 6 7 0	MaD aBouT BooKS
	M D B T B K S	My DeBT BaKeS

		My Dollars, But The Bank Keeps Some
Social Security	6 4 7 - 2 1 - 4 5 5 0	BRoKeN TRoLLeyS
	B R K N T R L L S	BRaKe oN TRoLLs
		Betsy Ross Knits Nifty Tees; Ross Loves Long Sleeves.
Safe combination	3 2 - 3 7 - 0 1	My NaMe KeyS iT
MoNey MaKeS iT	M N - M K - S T	Many Need Money, Kings Store Tons

In the Numbers-Converted-to-Letters System, you don't have to memorize a word substitute for every number up to a hundred or a thousand. If you found it easy to do that, you probably wouldn't need this system! Instead you memorize ten digit-consonant pairs and then construct memorable-to-you phrases or sentences with them at your leisure.

When you use the letter conversion to start a word, you may even be able to come up with verses for longer numbers. Here's an example made with the letters for the first twenty-one digits of pi. Using each letter as the first letter of a word, I came up with this bit of doggerel.

3. 1 4 1 5 9 2 6 5 3 5 8 9 7 9 3 2 3 8 4 6
M T R T L D N B L M L D P K P M N M D R B

Maxi's Taxi Raced Tim's Limo,
Driving Nimbly Between Lanes.
Maxi Lunged, Dinged a Porsche,
Knicked a Peugeot,
Missed a Nissan.
Maxi's Doctors Repaired Brain.

Obviously anything you come up with will be better, and the effort and pleasure you put into crafting your mnemonic will help fix your creation forever in your memory.

THE COUNTING-EQUIVALENT SYSTEM

There's another device for recalling numbers that takes more time than most want to spend to decode, but you might find it a pleasant diversion for long train journeys. You create a sentence or story in which the number of letters in each word is equal to the number itself. For example:

8—a word with 8 letters
5—a word with 5 letters
1—a 1-letter word
0—your name (or any other consistent, full-stop, attention-getting device!)

A classic use of this variant is the verse for remembering pi to the twenty-first digit:

Pie!
3
I wish I could determine pi.
1 4 1 5 9 2
Eureka, cried the great inventor.
6 5 3 5 8
Christmas pudding, Christmas pie
9 7 9 3
Is the problem's very center.
2 3 8 4 6

(The problem with this clever verse is that in it "pi" is also spelled "pie," but most people know that pi begins with a 3.)

This type of conversion takes some time to turn back into numbers, making it undesirable for numbers needed quickly on-the-hoof, like automated teller and phone numbers. But for data needed when filling out forms, it can serve very well.

THE PHONE-Y NUMBER SYSTEM

You can forget every other number system, if none of them has piqued your interest, but nearly everyone can use the Harvey Feinstein Phone-y Number System. My friend Harvey devised this simple trick many years ago for turning phone numbers into words. He discovered that most numbers could be turned into words by replacing each digit with one of the three letters of the alphabet that share the same number button. (These letters are holdovers from the golden days when every phone number began with a memorable "exchange"—PLaza 8, BEekman 2, MUrray Hill 3. Obviously the letters are no longer needed for that purpose, but then tradition changes slowly. Most of us still "dial" our push-button phones.)

Having dropped phone numbers containing letters in the name of efficiency, the phone companies soon realized that most people have a hard time remembering seven numbers. Phone mail systems often use the letters of employees' names. Recently "vanity" phone numbers have become available—for an extra charge. Businesses and organizations happily pay a premium for what they hope will be a memorable letter-number that will encourage calls, for instance 1-800-FLOWERS for a floral network, 1-800-PINDROP for a telephone service. With the Phone-y Number System, you can make your own mnemonics for free.

To use Harvey's system, write down the number you want to remember. Under each digit, write the three letters that also appear on that key. Try to spell out a word or words by selecting one letter for each number.

Here's what you see when you look at your telephone. (The numbers 0 and 1 have no letters, but substitutions are indicated in parentheses below.)

1 (Q or one)
2 A B C
3 D E F
4 G H I
5 J K L
6 M N O

7 P R S
8 T U V
9 W X Y
0 (Z or No!)

Harvey translated his own number into D-A-R-K-D-O-G (327-5364) and his girlfriend's was Y-O-U-L-O-V-E (968-5683).

CHECK THIS OUT

TURN PHONE-Y NUMBERS INTO WORDS

Choose some phone numbers you'd like to remember and write them down below. Under each number write the three possible letters. Here's an example:

Phone number	2	2	7	-	3	2	6	3
Possible letters	ABC	ABC	PRS	-	DEF	ABC	MNO	DEF
Some word	B	A	R		E	B	O	D
substitutes	C	A	P		E	C	O	D

"Bare bod" could refer to a Shakespeare lover (Hamlet's bare bodkin) or a friend who likes nude sunbathing. "Cape Cod" might remind you of experiences when you vacationed there, or of a fisherman or artist. Connect the phrase and the person. Here's another example:

Phone number	8	7	3	-	3	8	0	0
Possible letters	TUV	PRS	DEF	-	DEF	TUV	Z-NO!	Z-NO!
Some word	U	S	E		F	U	Z	Z
substitutes	T	R	E		E	T	NO!	NO!

The "fuzz" of "Use fuzz" could refer to peaches, beards, velvet, flocked wallpaper, or the slang term for police officers. "Treet" is misspelled, after which you cry, "No! No!" Perhaps this reminds you of an atrocious speller or someone who never picks up the check (treats) or a profession that treats people or products, such as a doctor or a rug cleaner. Once you find a word equivalent for the number, lock it to its owner with a strong visual or verbal image.

Now try some of your own. Use the same verbal skills you use for crossword puzzles to form words and phrases. Some phone numbers absolutely defy being turned into words, but enough work to make the system fun and useful. For your reference:

1	2	3	4	5	6	7	8	9	0
Q or one	ABC	DEF	GHI	JKL	MNO	PRS	TUV	WXY	Z or No!

Phone number ____ ____ ____ ____ ____ ____ ____
Possible letters ____ ____ ____ ____ ____ ____ ____
My word substitute ____ ____ ____ ____ ____ ____ ____

Phone number ____ ____ ____ ____ ____ ____ ____
Possible letters ____ ____ ____ ____ ____ ____ ____
My word substitute ____ ____ ____ ____ ____ ____ ____

Phone number ____ ____ ____ ____ ____ ____ ____
Possible letters ____ ____ ____ ____ ____ ____ ____
My word substitute ____ ____ ____ ____ ____ ____ ____

STRETCH YOUR DIGIT SPAN

In 1887, a London teacher named J. Jacobs wanted to see how well his students could recall long numbers. Each student was presented with ever-increasing sequences of digits and asked to repeat them. When a student could recall an entire string of numbers correctly half the time, this was his "digit span."[5] Today Jacobs's system for measuring number memory is a standard test for short-term memory ability. An average ten-year-old can repeat three out of five sequences of six numbers. The average twelve-year-old can repeat backward at least one of three series of five digits. The average adult can repeat two out of three series of seven numbers. Exceptional adults can do eight-digit sequences forward and seven-digit sequences backward.

It was long thought that someone's digit span was fairly well fixed and could be improved only slightly, if at all, by practice. However, in 1981 K. Anders Ericsson of the University of Colorado and William G. Chase of Carnegie-Mellon University decided to see if the digit span could be stretched.[6] They found a young volunteer with a normal digit span of seven and began testing and retesting him without giving him any instructions. Soon SF, as they called him, began to invent his own methods for recalling longer and longer strings of numbers. By the time they called it quits, SF had a digit span of 80! That is, he could listen to a string of 80 numbers and recall it correctly half the time.

How did he do it? It wasn't effortless. He spent an hour a day, three to five times a week, for twenty months recalling number sequences. That's 230 hours. For the first four sessions, his digit span was unchanged. During this time, he recalled the digit sequence by "rehearsing" it, saying it over and over to himself, either as a whole number or divided into two groups like a phone number. Sometimes he noticed patterns, like 246 or 987, but mostly he just tried to remember.

Then SF began to personalize the numbers. He was a competitive runner and easily remembered running times from his long-term memory. At session five, he began relating the digit strings to things he already knew. The number cluster 3.492 could represent 3 minutes, 49.2 seconds, an impressive time for running a mile. The number 893 became 89.3 years, an impressive age for a runner. After the first hundred hours of practice, SF took only half the time to memorize a specific number of digits.

SF's final strategy was to structure large numbers into smaller groups, each containing three, four, or five digits. To remember the 80-digit number, he used this pattern:

4-4-4 4-4-4 3-3-3 3-3-3 4-4-4 3-3-3 4-4-4 5

Even if you're not a runner, you probably have dozens, maybe hundreds, of number sequences you already know to use as memory pegs for recalling new numbers: birthdays, historical dates, phone numbers, addresses, important dates in your own life.

SF's success illustrates that average people can have extraordinary recall when they use strategies. The strategies become even more powerful when they are personalized to use what people already know. A 1993 study at the University of Utah indicated that people are most successful when they invent and use their own encoding system: "Self-generated mnemonics." A group of 164 volunteers, ranging in age from twenty to eighty-six, were given number lists to memorize. The younger subjects, those under forty-nine, were more likely to report that they had come up with a system for remembering. They also recalled more numbers.[7] This may be because we tend to be more adaptable, curious, and willing to make mistakes when we are younger.

CHECK THIS OUT

TEST YOUR DIGIT SPAN

As you've just seen, a digit span seems to indicate an inborn ability *but* it can also be dramatically increased with effort.

If you'd like to know your current digit span, here's how to find it. Have someone read you four-digit numbers, until it is clear that you can repeat them correctly more than half the time.

Or, if you're alone and have a tape recorder, type or write a column of fifty random four-digit numbers in a column on a sheet of paper. Slide a piece of plain paper down the page, revealing each four-digit number one at a time. Glance at the number just above your masking sheet, glance away and repeat it aloud into the tape recorder, then reveal the next number. When you're done, check your recorded answers against the answers on the typed page.

If you have repeated more than half of the four-digit numbers correctly, move on to five-digit, six-digit, seven-digit numbers, and so forth. Increase the quantity of digits until your success rate drops below 50 percent. The highest number of digits that you remember correctly more than half the time is your digit span. That is, if you could remember seven digits more than half the time but eight digits less than half the time, then seven is your digit span. Seven is regarded as average. A few people can recall ten digits.

Would you feel enriched and more powerful if you increased your digit span? Would it be worth the effort needed? If so, go for it! There's no proof (yet) that using memory systems causes any changes in the brain's innate ability to remember, but there is definite proof that people who use systems remember more.

CHECK THIS OUT

Review Time

Go back and review the way you linked the names of the presidents of the United States in Day 3. You'll probably be pleasurably surprised at the results!

DAY 6

How to Remember What You Read

WHAT YOU'LL LEARN IN THIS CHAPTER

- How your brain processes and remembers written information
- The power of previewing and adapting to different densities of text
- How to use the Five Nonfiction Structures to recall more of what you read

With billions of printed words clamoring for our attention, promising to make us richer, smarter, and happier, many people want to run their eyes over a page and have the words permanently installed in their long-term memory. It is a kind of "magic thinking" that evolved during childhood when reading often meant studying. "When I grow up," we reasoned, "I'll never have to study again, but I'll remember everything I read."

There *is* a grown-up secret to remembering more of what you read as an adult, but it has nothing to do with superior mental powers or forcing yourself to work harder. The secret to remembering what you read is recognizing *structures*.

The normal mind's natural inclination—its greatest strength and its greatest weakness, too—is to create structure out of random bits of information. We want to have an effect for every cause, a number three after every number two, a moral for every occurrence. We try to turn events into stories, nature into landscapes. In the real world, this isn't always possible, but fortunately in the world of the written word, structure is part of the process of presenting information.

An ancient said that with a lever big enough and something to stand on, he could move the earth. Similarly, with logical (but flexible) structures, you can process and store unlimited information. Consider, for instance, that with only a little effort and unlimited time, you could easily write out every number between 1 and 100 trillion in order, using the structure called counting. Media philosopher Richard Saul Wurman says, "accessibility is made possible by the discovery of a structure."[1] When you create structures for noticing and storing what you read, you can snatch up relevant bits as you go and file them as fast as you encounter them.

What are the benefits of processing information more efficiently that can lure you to change comfortable lifelong habits? When I ask students in my reading workshops what they hope to achieve, their typical replies are

- "I would get through three times as many of the books and magazines I should read and really be on top of things."
- "By being more efficient, getting through the compulsory stuff faster, I'd have more time left over to do the things I enjoy."
- "I'd be happy just to stop falling further and further behind!"

HOW FAST SHOULD YOU READ?

Reading efficiently often means reading quickly, keeping your mind alert and focused. However, this chapter is not about "speed reading." It is about adjusting your processing methods to the kind of material you are reading and what you want to get out of it.

Efficient processing doesn't mean you have to give up traditional slow reading. There are tremendous benefits to reading some things slowly, savoring every nuance and detail. Who'd want to race through love letters, contracts, wills, or an IRS return? Some reading is actually done best word for word.

Processing printed words slowly also provides us with a way to shut out the world, to slow down, to go into a trance-like state of total absorption. There's even another benefit attached to reading slowly. What do some people do to fall asleep? Right. They read!

Reading yourself to sleep is only a problem when that isn't your intention. Have you ever been running your eyes over print and suddenly noticed that you haven't the slightest idea what the last few paragraphs were about? Your mind wandered. Chances are you spent years in school allowing your mind to wander. What else can a mind do when it thinks faster than it is informed?

The human mind can process at least 800 words a minute.[2] So why do most intelligent people read about 250 words a minute? Because that's as fast as we can talk or say the words in our heads. Some of us were taught to read accurately and precisely, *word for word*. Slower readers are still busy saying each word and hearing its sound echoing in their heads. That's wonderful for Shakespeare and the more colorful sportswriters, but not for the masses of nuts-and-bolts information we encounter every day.

BEATING COMPUTERS

Efficient readers get through the daily information onslaught by borrowing some techniques from computers. They learn to recognize common structures for information and to search for key words and ideas, soaring high over unrelated material and zooming down to focus on the desired bit. But computers are never bored. They just do mechanically what they've been told to do. People need both pleasure and purpose to work efficiently, and slow down considerably when they become bored.

Fortunately efficient human information processors are rarely bored because they are *active*. They make themselves curious and excited about the glut of facts, figures, and ideas they encounter, by constantly asking questions, answering them, and then formulating new questions as they go. Their efficiency comes from racing ahead eagerly, not from being shoved from behind.

CHECK THIS OUT

Your Reading Priorities

Start by writing down the kind of reading that creates problems when you don't do it, the kind you wish you had more time for, or that you never seem to get to.

I Have Problems When I Don't Read

1. ______________________________
2. ______________________________
3. ______________________________
4. ______________________________

Keep going if you need to. Then make a list of the ten things you are most interested in in the world, things that may or may not have anything to do with the reading you want or need to do.

The Ten Things That Interest Me Most

1. ______________________________
2. ______________________________
3. ______________________________
4. ______________________________
5. ______________________________
6. ______________________________
7. ______________________________
8. ______________________________
9. ______________________________
10. ______________________________

Do any of the items on your first list fall under the categories on your second list? If not, are you willing to replace one of your ten high-interest categories with a new one that includes the reading you want to do? Remember that as an intelligent person, *you* are in charge of what you choose to miss. *You* decide what it is reasonable to know. Of course society and your teachers and employers are going to try to influence your choices, but you are the final judge. As long as you feel that others are making choices for you, you will resist and experience overload, no matter how small or simple the actual volume. When you see yourself in charge, energized by your inborn curiosity and able to decide what to notice and what to ignore, "overload" becomes an impossibility.

HOW USEFUL IS ANXIETY?

Anxiety is a powerful personal energizer. Some people choose to use it instead of curiosity or joy as a source of adrenaline for their daily tasks. Being chronically in "overload" can become a safe way to feel. It is familiar and comfortable, "a poor thing but mine own."

Let's do an anxiety check.

I should read more:	No Guilt	Some Anxiety	Lots of Anxiety
1. ______________________	[ ]	[ ]	[ ]
2. ______________________	[ ]	[ ]	[ ]
3. ______________________	[ ]	[ ]	[ ]
4. ______________________	[ ]	[ ]	[ ]
5. ______________________	[ ]	[ ]	[ ]

If your mind is temporarily blank, here are some subjects frequently mentioned by participants in my seminars:

job, business	retirement plans
world events	health issues
sports	the performing arts
gossip	special-interest action groups
election issues	personal interests
new legislation	

What do *you* choose to feel guilty about? Is this anxiety useful to you? That is, does it motivate you to find more efficient ways to process all this information? Or does it stall you and make you feel helpless, useless, totally overwhelmed?

Is it possible you have a choice about how you process information?	[ ] yes	[ ] no
Is it possible that you have a choice about how much you remember?	[ ] yes	[ ] no

If you answered yes to either of these questions, keep reading.

READING WITHOUT GUILT?

Comedian Woody Allen claimed he learned to speed-read *War and Peace* in five minutes. When someone asked him what it was about, he replied "Russia." If you shudder when you encounter real-life versions of racing through fiction looking for facts, so do I. Fiction is meant to seduce. It is rarely created to provide clumps or sequences of useful, bare-bones information. Most of the reading we want to recall is nonfiction that can be compared to K rations, relatively tasteless, but full of essential nutrients. Fiction, on the other hand, may be either rare wine or junk food, but it is meant to be tasted, not swallowed whole. To switch metaphors, fiction represents the footpaths, not the highways of the printed word. So abandon any sense of guilt as you stroll through novels and poems.

Unfortunately, the simple act of reading has the potential for providing many sources of guilt. We can feel guilty that we don't read more "meaningful" books or that we haven't read the latest best-seller that everyone is talking about. We can feel guilty that we spend too much time reading or that we don't spend enough. We can feel guilty that we don't get enough out of what we read, or that we can't remember it later as well as we would like to, or that we simply can't understand the instructions that come with a new VCR or digital watch or answering machine.

Sometimes we feel so guilty about what we *should* be reading, that we fill our shelves with unread magazines, journals, and books, or subscribe to special-interest book clubs, or join groups that meet regularly to discuss a book that everyone (ideally) has read, then drop out because we never get around to reading the chosen book. The opportunity to discuss the ideas in books with others can be a heady and illuminating pastime, but it shouldn't turn into a restriction or yet another source of guilt. Doris Lessing, in *The Golden Notebook*, says,

> *There is only one way to read, which is to browse through libraries and book shops, picking up books that attract you, reading only those, dropping them when they bore you, skipping the parts that drag—and never, never reading anything because you feel you ought, or because it is part of a trend or a movement. Remember that the book that bores you when you are twenty or thirty will open doors for you when you are forty or fifty—and vice versa. Don't read a book out of its right time for you.*[3]

This is deliciously true for pleasure reading (and that can be anything from a Harlequin romance to a treatise on fifth-century Irish plainsong), but the "real world" of compulsory reading intrudes too often. To survive and thrive in our professions, communities, or civilization, it is necessary to know what is happening when and who is doing what to whom. *This* is the kind of information that structured information processing is designed to conquer.

Old Injunctions	New Permissions
Don't miss a word.	Read for ideas, not words.
Start at the beginning.	Begin wherever your interest takes you.
Finish what you start.	Take what you want and leave the rest.
Never mark a book.	Mark your own books if you like.
Read only after you finish your real work.	Reading is thinking—read in prime time.

REMEMBERING FICTION

Obviously I have a powerful bias against reading fiction for anything but personal enhancement, but sooner or later you're going to be in a literature class. Here you will meet many exciting new friends on the written page, but this sublime experience is nearly always followed by a *test*. Since education must be measurable, you will have to prove that you have actually read and absorbed the material. If you're fortunate, this test will be in the form of an essay on what you have experienced in the company of this author. If you're not, this will be a multiple-choice test in which you must recall character names, obscure plot points, and quite likely an opinion of the work offered by the teacher or the textbook author.

Resign yourself, content in the knowledge that this public exercise is separate from your private affair with the author. Figure out what the teacher wants to see on your test paper and use the techniques in this book to commit these points to memory. Make flash cards, write a synopsis, create a cast list and jot personal notes after each name. Analyze themes and premises, action and resolution. Your appreciation may be increased by these efforts, but if overanalysis starts to erode your enthusiasm, remember that you are free to abandon this critical approach and return to pure enjoyment once the class is over. Converting great literature to boxes on a test paper is like converting great music to jagged lines on an oscilloscope. You always have the power to convert it back.

A NEW READING APPROACH

You don't need to know everything. You don't even need to *read* everything. To use structural information processing, you must develop a healthy disrespect for the printed word. Your need to know and your own goals must supersede those of the author.

Of all the other communications skills, reading is most like listening. You don't hang on every word when most people talk to you. Be just as selective when you listen to an author talking to you through the printed page as you are when you listen to a voice on the radio.

Once you give yourself permission to choose what you need and want to absorb, and to let the other stuff go (while knowing where to look for it if you change your mind), you have made your first big step toward remembering what you read. This doesn't mean that you block out everything that doesn't fit a limited vision of the world. Rather, you stay aware of the swirling background of information while you focus on what is relevant to you. You remain open to changing or expanding your area of concentration, but you don't try to have it all.

HOW YOU PERCEIVE WHAT YOU READ

"When *I* use a word," says Humpty Dumpty in Lewis Carroll's *Through the Looking-Glass,* "it means just what I choose it to mean—neither more nor less." In my reading workshops I use a series of perception exercises that I call the *Humpty Dumpty Experiments*. They are designed to make people aware of how they process written information.

CHECK THIS OUT

HUMPTY DUMPTY EXPERIMENT I

How Do You Read?

Before you can train yourself to recall more of what you read, you need to understand the mechanics of *how* you read. For *this exercise only,* get out a watch or clock with a second hand and time yourself. How long does it take you to read each of the four columns below? Jot the time in the space below each column.

I	hand	"History is	To be or not to be:
D	bird	the fiction	that is the question;
H	cage	we invent	Whether 'tis nobler
W	pots	to persuade	in the mind to suffer
X	lady	ourselves that	the slings and arrows
N	both	events are	of outrageous fortune,
M	jump	knowable and	or to take arms against
O	star	that life	a sea of troubles, and
P	flop	has order and	by opposing end them?
E	surf	direction.	To die: to sleep no
A	gist	That's why	more; and, by a
Z	isle	events	sleep to say we end
G	aunt	are always	the heartache and
H	prop	reinterpreted	the thousand natural
P	film	when values	shocks that flesh is
I	back	change. We	heir to, 'tis a
T	fore	need new	consummation devoutly
E	gasp	versions	to be wish'd. To die,
Q	sink	of history	to sleep; To sleep:
S	ores	to allow for	perchance to dream: ay,
F	bind	our current	there's the rub; For
H	poor	prejudices."	in that sleep of death
K	fuzz	The philosophy	what dreams may come,
M	nose	of Calvin, as	when we have shuffled
N	mind	set forth in	off this mortal coil,
C	sick	Bill Watterson's	must give us pause.
X	tape	droll comic strip	There's the respect
Z	ship	*Calvin and*	that makes calamity
B	fish	*Hobbes,*	of so long life; For
U	hair	July 19, 1993.	who would . . .
____ seconds	____ seconds	____ seconds	____ seconds
Column 1 has 30 letters	Column 2 has 30 words	Column 3 has 60 words	Column 4 has 120 words

Notice that column 2 has four times as many letters as column 1, but it didn't take you four times as long to read. Most people read columns 1 and 2 in about the same time. That's because we can read words just as quickly as letters. Then notice that column 3 contains twice the words as column 2, but is easier to read because it has meaning. And column 4 may have been the easiest to read, because you were familiar with the material. Probably, as soon as you realized you were reading Hamlet's Act III soliloquy, you just glanced at the whole thing to make sure it was there as you remembered it.

A caricature sketch represents a complex whole with a few lines. We recognize it and our brains fill in the rest of the picture. Reading is much like looking at a line drawing. We never actually read every word or even every sentence. Our mind races along looking for signposts, while knowledge of basic word and sentence structures lets us fill in the blanks.

Letters and words are only symbols. Like Humpty Dumpty, we supply the meaning, and when we do that, we are halfway to filing the information in our personalized memory storage structures.

HUMPTY DUMPTY EXPERIMENT II

Reading What's Not There

In the following story, every fourth word has been dropped. See if you can still get the gist of the story. Take as long as you wish, but try to move through it smoothly, with a pleasurable curiosity.

What constitutes "intelligence" ______ considerably from culture ______ culture, even among ______ within a single ______. Obviously all parents ______ to prepare their ______ for maximum potential ______ in our difficult ______. But which world? ______ skills and talents ______ to be maximized ______ which ignored or ______ suppressed? Each cultural ______ teaches its children ______ respond as intelligently ______ possible to given ______. When one group ______ that another is ______ intelligent or is "______ smart for its ______ good," it is ______ to judge it ______ its own standards. "______ are N.L.U." (Not ______ Us!")

Now ask yourself:

The subject of this paragraph is ______________________________.

The author's opinion is ______________________________

______________________________.

(*Answers are at the end of this chapter.*)

The more familiar you become with any subject, the easier it is to grasp information from the barest outline. Efficient readers can often use their knowledge of the shapes and sizes of words to make sense of illegible handwriting, blurred print, and obliterated text. Here's an example in which one letter of the typewriter got stuck. Can you still read it?

Evxryonx Can Makx a Diffxrxncx

Whxnxvxr you arx txmptxd to givx up and say, "What diffxrxncx could I xvxr makx? I'm just onx pxrson," rxmxmbxr that xxtraordinary pxrson Xlxanor Roosxvxlt. Shx was inatxly shy, quitx homxly, and raisxd to bx a rxtiring wifx and mothxr, but shx ovxrcamx hxr own fxars and dxficixncixs to bxcomx an outspokxn and bxlovxd spokxspxrson for thx rights of pxoplx xvxrywhxrx. Whxn shx dixd, Adlai Stxvxnson said: "I havx lost a frixnd. I havx lost an inspiration. Shx would rathxr light candlxs than cursx thx darknxss and hxr glow has warmxd thx world."

Which letter stuck? This little tale illustrates another aspect of memory: that it is important to make errors in order to improve recall. You may have decided on the meaning of a word and then realized, a sentence later, that your first guess didn't make sense. Does that make you remember less well? Or does the active process of determination improve your recall later? Bright people discover how to stay flexible, to realize that something isn't working, and to back up and try again. That's not failing. That's being smart.

THE MOST EFFICIENT READING STRATEGIES

There are two extraordinarily simple strategies that can double your "reading comprehension" without effort. In fact, both are things you already do naturally, unless your teachers succeeded in curbing such "misbehavior." They are

1. Read at a variable speed
2. Preview

Reading studies reported by Richard Wagner and Robert J. Sternberg in 1987 found that highly efficient readers don't read faster or with greater effort than ordinary readers, but they "have the intelligence to know what to read and how to read it. [He or she is] a master of time allocation and wastes no time responding inappropriately."[4] This is the same approach that I've been encouraging for the past fifteen years.

Perhaps your grade school teachers, coping with students at different reading levels, struggled valiantly to keep you all on the same page. Reading at a consistent speed and "knowing the place" became more important than remembering what you read. Happily, you can now discard this old injunction and read the way that feels right because it *is* right.

You absorb information most efficiently when you give yourself permission to read at different speeds. Start by flying high over what you already know. Whenever something stands out that is different, swoop down and examine it. This lets you use the structure of what you already know to notice and file new information.

Another childhood injunction to discard is "Don't look ahead." There you were, eager to flip through the entire book, but that was often discouraged. Your new instruction is to preview long articles and books before you start. Previewing gives you a lot back for very little energy.

Anytime you set out on a trip, a map helps you to get an idea of the distances and terrain. Previewing is like scanning a map. You look over the territory to see how long the journey will be, how simple or complicated.

By *pre*viewing reading material, you may find signposts in the form of headings and chapter names. The lengths of the paragraphs will provide clues to how thickly packed the ideas are. Lots of short paragraphs usually mean lots of different ideas but fewer supporting details. Long paragraphs hint at fewer ideas but lots of supporting data.

There are two big advantages to previewing material:

1. Familiarizing yourself with the material before reading makes it possible to read it faster later. When you absorb even a little of it, going through it again is easier because we are all more secure with "familiar" material. The recognizable landmarks increase your motivation, and your mind is less likely to wander. You are reading with a goal in mind.
2. You may learn all you need to know from the headings, pictures, and charts. You may even decide you don't need to read the material after all.

Your memory reading strategies start with giving yourself permission to read at your own speed and to look ahead before you start.

WHAT DO YOU CHOOSE TO NOTICE?

You make thousands, even millions of decisions each day about what to notice and what to ignore. You might compare the average day to a train ride: You can stare out the window, talk to other passengers, notice the rhythms and operations of the vehicle. A wide variety of information is available for you to choose from.

You face similar choices in what you choose to run your eyes over (staring out the window versus staring at the upholstery design, looking at the distant mountains versus looking at the nearby trees) and what you choose to retain.

Imagine that you are going through a huge pile of your daily mail, feeling really overloaded. Which of the following would catch your attention and register:

[ ] Dear Sir or Madam,

Have you ever considered the value of owning a really fine set of encyclopedias . . .

[ ] Dear Penelope J. Peat,

You may already have won $1 million! Please take a minute to fill out the enclosed response card and . . .

[ ] Dear Ms. Peat,

Your uncle, William Dillon Peat III, died on May 3 of this year and has named you in his will. If you will call my office . . .

[ ] The Annual Hanson High School Reunion Bash will be held this year at the Kiwanis Hall on June 15. This year's theme will be "Your Cheatin' Heart." Come as your favorite country and western singer . . .

[ ] Sir:

Our records show that we have not received your quarterly payment of $101.23. If we do not receive it by November 1, we will be forced to cancel your auto insurance . . .

Which of those messages did you reject by dropping the letter in the wastebasket? Which got your attention? Obviously *any* of them could be meaningful or extraneous. Most people would ignore the sales pitches and zero in on the letter about an inheritance. But perhaps you've been planning to buy an encyclopedia and you know that Uncle Bill was a deadbeat who probably left you his pet flea collection. The auto insurance letter should trigger a response, unless you just sold your car and have taken up roller skating to work. Are you starting to see that you have *choices* about noticing? About responding?

CHECK THIS OUT

HUMPTY DUMPTY EXPERIMENT III

Filling in Missing Pieces

Sometimes the author hasn't given you all the information you need. Actively filling in missing pieces is a powerful aide to recalling the information later. See if you can spot the missing pieces in these three brief paragraphs:

> Great Britain dominates the world of "privatization" with the government pocketing $29.41 billion since its program to sell off state-owned assets began in 1979. But Britain was hardly alone in its efforts. Total proceeds in 1993 from government sales of assets amounted to $43 billion.

What else would you like to know to form a value judgment about this information?

____

____

____

(Notice how asking yourself questions and filling in missing pieces can make even dull information more memorable.)

> We have transferred your loan to the XYZ Company. In the future, make all your payments to their Cincinnati office, Att: Car Loans. Don't use the payment coupons you have now.

What else would you like to know before you can carry out these instructions?

Lenin was persecuted for his political beliefs. Since the Russian revolution in 1917, many Russians came to America fleeing communism.

Both these sentences are correct. Do you suspect that some information may be missing? What else would you like to know before concluding that Lenin fled to America to escape communism?

(*Answers are at the end of this chapter.*)

You've explored how your brain perceives words, how it can grasp whole phrases and ideas as quickly as single words, while remembering much more. Now discover how you perceive larger chunks of information.

CHECK THIS OUT

HUMPTY DUMPTY EXPERIMENT IV

Identifying Information Chunks

Here is a Fact Hunt.

First, browse casually, as you'd peruse a magazine in a dentist's office. Slow down if anything catches your attention.

ZZZ

There's nothing sleepy about Z! It is a descendent of *zayin,* the seventh letter of the Hebrew alphabet, which came from the Phoenician word for "weapon." In its early form it looked like a capital I or sword.

The Greeks changed the letter to the unique shape we now know and called it *zeta,* which also stood for the number seven. Their god Zeus was fond of Z-shaped lightning bolts.

The Romans rarely used Z except to indicate the Greek *zeta* in words borrowed from that language, and they consigned it to the end of the Latin alphabet.

When the French language evolved from Latin, using the same alphabet, the letter was called both "zed" and "zee." Although the English call the letter "zed," and the Italians and Spaniards still say "zeta," the current American pronunciation is from the French "zee."

Today we esteem Zn (zinc) and Zr (zirconium). In mathematics, Z is often the third unknown, such as in X, Y, and Z. And when we want to convey a delightful completeness, we say, "from A to Z."

Now read ZZZ again, this time with intense curiosity. Be eager to collect and remember as many of the details as possible. (If the subject doesn't interest you, pretend that you're about to pose questions on this article to someone you dislike.) When you have finished, answer the questions below.

QUESTIONS

1. The first letter Z was shaped like ____________________.
2. *Zayin* was the seventh letter of the Hebrew alphabet.
   ( ) true   ( ) false
3. The Romans used Z
   ( ) only in equations.
   ( ) only in words of Greek origin.
4. Today the English call the letter ____________
   while Italians and Spaniards say ____________
   but Americans pronounce it ____________.

5. Z originated in Hebrew and reached English by a path through what three other languages?

(*Answers are at the end of this chapter.*)

Notice how different each process feels. Were you energized and excited after the casual reading of Step 1? Probably not. Was it uncomfortable to focus your attention, even for the brief time necessary, in Step 2? Probably so. As you hone your structural skills, you are going to get more and more comfortable with this active approach.

CHECK THIS OUT

HUMPTY DUMPTY EXPERIMENT V

Identifying Main Ideas

You've practiced looking for words and spotting facts. This time you are going to practice finding *ideas*. Often the main idea of a book, article, or letter doesn't pop out at once. The writer has positioned it after a lot of exposition, justifications, or background. Read the following, looking for the main idea.

PROGRESS

(1) Most of us have grown up believing in our place in a world with ever-expanding opportunities. **(2)** "Progress"—the right to a better education, better health care, a better job, and a higher standard of living—has seemed a given. **(3)** Tales of past hardships from parents and grandparents have seemed as remote as the Peloponnesian War. **(4)** But now some experts are predicting that we will be the first American generation since the 1930s that can't expect to live better than its parents did. **(5)** The perks of civilization, like free libraries and parks, are being cut back sharply. **(6)** Even essentials like hospitals, roads, bridges, fire and police protection, and schools are threatened. **(7)** A volatile economy is confronting us daily with unfamiliar and intimidating challenges. **(8)** It's easy to feel betrayed.

QUESTIONS

The sentence containing the main idea is ______________________.
The sentences that support this idea are ______________________.

Your initial impulse in response to the first question may have been to choose the first sentence, because you were taught in school that it must contain the main idea. Your second choice may have been the second sentence, because it contained the word "progress," which is also the title of the piece. (Headings can be misleading.) Actually the main idea doesn't come until sentence **(4)**: ". . . some experts are predicting that we will be the first American generation since the 1930s that can't expect to live better than its parents did." Every sentence before **(4)** is positioning the reader for the bad news to come. Every sentence after **(4)** is a support for or effect of the statement.

The so-called rules about opening each paragraph with a main-idea sentence may work in short encyclopedia entries, but not in the real world of ideas and language. People just don't write or think like that. Main ideas often lurk in the middle or at the very end of a paragraph, article, or book. Sometimes the main point must even be inferred—for instance, an article on what happens when pregnant women use crack cocaine may offer many tragic examples but never state directly that "crack hurts babies."

Some authors actually put two main ideas in one paragraph. Find the two ideas in the following passage.

STENCILS

(1) It's hard to love a stencil. **(2)** To begin with, it is usually made of second-rate materials like paper, cardboard, or cheap metal. **(3)** Then, once used, it's messy, covered with sticky guck and requires a special place to dry. **(4)** Even today stencils are one of the least-used means of transferring designs. **(5)** Although stencils are one of mankind's oldest marking devices, early civilizations soon replaced them with the more elegant and efficient seal. **(6)** Seals were used on every kind of surface to mark possessions and products. **(7)** The Egyptians used seals shaped like scarabs (beetles), which were carved from soapstone and often worn as jewelry. **(8)** Romans loved their signet rings. **(9)** Renaissance guilds were required to mark their goods, and there was even a law passed in 1266 that required English bakers to stamp every loaf of bread with both their guild seal and a description of the contents. **(10)** In an age of illiteracy, every monarch had a seal so he could sign his name. **(11)** Seals were much more satisfying than mere stencils, much more macho. **(12)** Can you imagine Nero suggestively stroking his stencil while leering at a scantily clad dancing girl?

QUESTIONS:

The two main ideas are in sentence ______(supported by sentences ______) and sentence ______ (supported by sentences ______).

(*Answers are at the end of this chapter.*)

Learning to recognize the main ideas quickly is the first step in filing information for later recall. Think of the page as three-dimensional. If it is well written, the key idea should pop out at you, with supports and details lining up in the background. Once you identify the main idea, you are free to race from paragraph to paragraph, spotting what you want to know and reading the supporting examples only if you choose to. All writing is composed of *generalizations* and *details*. For example:

Generalization: composers

Details: Bach, Beethoven, Bellini, Bernstein, Brahms, Chopin, Dubin, Gershwin, Gounod, Kern, Lennon, Liszt, Loesser, McCartney, Mendelssohn, Monteverdi, Mozart, Porter, Puccini, Rachmaninoff, Ravel, Rodgers, Romberg, Schubert, Sondheim, Sting, Stravinsky, Verdi, Weber

The generalization is often (but not always) the subject of the passage, while the details are supports.

THE FIVE NONFICTION PATTERNS

Remembering fiction is strictly between you and the author. It is a sensuous private interaction where your memories are as much of your own mental images and emotional responses as of the author's words.

Remembering nonfiction is what most people mean when they say, "I want to remember what I read." We want to get more from newspapers, books, technical journals, newsletters, textbooks, and instructions the first time we read them, without having to go over and over them. The simple way to do this is to recognize the structure of what we are reading and then mentally to sort and file informational chunks under the appropriate headings as we go.

Patterns are the basis of memory. Edward de Bono says:

Once a pattern has been formed, then the mind no longer has to analyze or sort information. All that is required is enough information to trigger the pattern. The mind then follows along the pattern automatically in the same way a driver follows a familiar road. So any vague movement is instantly treated as an approaching vehicle. There is another important characteristic of the patterning system of the mind. Unless there are competing patterns, then anything remotely similar to the established pattern will be treated just as if it were that pattern.[5]

Fortunately most nonfiction information comes in one of five different patterns or structures:

Problem
Instruction
Information
Opinion
Thesis

Nearly all nonfiction falls into one of these five patterns. By learning to recognize and identify these five patterns as you read, you can find what you are looking for quickly and remember it more easily. (Occasionally you will run across a hybrid—a combination of two different patterns—or material that is so badly written you have no idea what the author intended. Strategies for dealing with both will be covered later.)

When you don't have any particular need to know, it's easy to fall into your old habit of just passing your eyes from left to right over each line.

You end up with a random collection of miscellaneous ideas and impressions, and that's fine when you are reading strictly for pleasure. But suppose that's not your purpose. If you want to process information efficiently, but you haven't yet decided exactly what you want to come away with for your effort, start by analyzing the *structure* of what you're reading.

The Problem Pattern—To spark action
Problem
Effects
Causes
Solution

The Instruction Pattern—To instruct
Materials (optional)
Step 1
Step 2
Step 3, etc.

The Information Pattern—To share information
Facet 1
Facet 2
Facet 3, etc.

The Opinion Pattern—To persuade
Opinion
Reasons
Significance

The Thesis Pattern—To prove something
Thesis
Proofs
Implications

When you walk into a hotel in a strange city, you can usually find the registration desk, the elevator, and your room, once you have the room number, because you recognize a familiar structure. And when you buy a new car or stereo, the controls may be in slightly different locations, but you can still figure out how to operate them. The details may be different, but the overall patterns are the same.

In the same way, you can be in control of noticing and remembering what you read when you can recognize the five nonfiction patterns.

The Problem Pattern—To spark action
Problem
Effects
Causes
Solution

The Problem Pattern is probably the most important nonfiction form because of its power to change how we perceive and do things. Some of the most important books of each century fall into this category: Consider the social and political impact of Emile Zola's *J'accuse* or Rachel Carson's *The Silent Spring*. You know you're looking at a Problem Pattern when you find answers to these questions:

Is there a problem? (What's wrong?)
What are the effects? (How do we know there's a problem?)
What are the causes? (Why is this happening?)
Solutions (What can we do about it?)

Is there a problem? Yes! How do we know? Because of all these unfortunate effects. And why is there a problem? Because of the following reasons. And what should be done about it? The author offers a solution.

As soon as you suspect you are reading about a problem, make a mental statement about it: "The problem is . . ." Then look for the causes, effects, and solutions. Everything else is just supporting detail and entertaining asides for the four structural points.

What if you were wrong and it turns out that the author isn't discussing a problem after all? You haven't wasted any effort. Your active reading has still made the material memorable and eliminated one of the five structural possibilities.

The Instruction Pattern—To instruct
Materials (optional)
Step 1
Step 2
Step 3, etc.

Anything that starts with "How to" is probably an example of the Instruction Pattern. Instructions can tell us how to do anything from electrical wiring to world travel. Look for numbered steps, or for words like "first," "second," "then," and "next."

Manufacturers and government agencies spend millions of dollars on instructions, yet some people can't program their VCRs or fill out the "easy" tax forms. Whose fault is it? Often the instructions aren't written clearly, but sometimes, even before they start, readers have already convinced themselves that they will not be able to understand. They run their eyes quickly down the page and just as quickly give up.

Instructions *can* be intimidating. Many have to be read slowly and carefully, one step at a time. If they are poorly written, you may have to rewrite them in your mind to make them comprehensible. Most of us will put extra effort into understanding and remembering instructions for something we find pleasurable, while we resist those that seem irrelevant or threatening. This is a conscious choice. Just remember that *not* reading instructions for things like medications, electrical appliances, or payment schedules can cost time, money, maybe even your life.

The Information Pattern—To share information
Facet 1
Facet 2
Facet 3, etc.

The Information Pattern consists of lots of facts about something. While the author may be enthusiastic about the subject (have an opinion about it) and may even describe some problems related to it, the primary purpose of the piece is to tell you lots of different facts.

The trick to structuring and storing great quantities of facts and figures is to divide the material into topical sections as you read. Each section represents a different facet of the main subject. Sometimes the author has already arranged the facets in a structure—by time, by location, by category. Even better, each category may have a headline identifying the facet. But sometimes you have to do the work for the writer, sorting facets yourself.

M.I.T. professor Marvin Minsky describes the heart of the M.I.T. structural approach to information:

If we ask . . . about the common everyday structures—that which a person needs to have ordinary common sense—we will find first a collection of indispensable categories, each rather complex: geometrical and mechanical properties of things and of space; uses and properties of a few thousand objects; hundreds of "facts" about hundreds of people, thousands of facts about tens of people, tens of facts about thousands of people; hundreds of facts about hundreds of organizations. As one tries to classify all his knowledge, the categories grow rapidly at first, but after a while, one encounters more and more difficulty. . . .[6]

Suddenly there are too many categories, some overlapping each other, and some sort of simplification is essential. Just as new technologies are generally enormously complex at first and then are simplified, so our information systems first grow more and more intricate and then more and more simple, depending on our need to distinguish. For example, rats, termites, and wasps are quite different, but for the purposes of inspiring a call to the exterminator they can all assume the common group status of "pests."

Poor writing can actually provide advantages for the structural information processor. When you spot a bit of information that is out of place, you have to review the facets that you have already filed in your mental structure so you can plop the out-of-place bit in the right hole. This strengthens your grasp of the parts and the whole.

Fortunately most authors (or their editors) have seen to it that information is being presented in a logical structure. If you are not provided with subheadings as road signs, become sensitive to whenever the author changes the treatment of the subject. It usually means that a new facet is beginning. In my classroom exercises, students read actual newspaper and magazine articles, putting a pencil slash wherever the author switches to a new facet, then going back and writing a heading for each section. Teach yourself to do this in your head as you read. This is what the Information Pattern is all about.

The Opinion Pattern—To persuade
Opinion
Reasons
Significance

The Opinion Pattern is sometimes hard to distinguish from the Problem or Thesis Patterns in the first few paragraphs or pages. Any writers offering a Problem Pattern or Thesis Pattern piece are automatically expressing an opinion. In their opinions, there is a problem or an important new way to evaluate something. You can identify an Opinion Pattern piece more by what is missing than by what is present. The pure Opinion Pattern offers *no* proposed solutions (essential for the Problem Pattern) and *no* originality of opinion supported by scientific proofs (both essential for the Thesis Pattern).

Why is it so important to recognize an Opinion Pattern when you see it? Because when you do, you won't read an opinion piece as if it were fact or "hard news." Editorial bias can be present in the most innocent phrasing or juxtaposition of articles on a newspaper page. Be an informed consumer of print!

Don't be tricked by patterns in disguise. Most newspapers and journals contain both news stories and commentary, and it is all too easy to accept an opinion as something it isn't. Here are your danger signals.

Opinion Masquerading as Information

1. The information is obviously incomplete and/or open to other interpretations.
2. The author's observations are very personal and subjective.

Opinion Masquerading as Problem

1. The author offers an observation rather than a solution.
2. The reasons for the opinion don't represent causes or effects of a problem.

Opinion Masquerading as Thesis

1. The writer states a proposition but supports it with opinions instead of facts.
2. The supports cannot be confirmed. (For example, the data is anecdotal or cannot be replicated; or the sources of the quotes or figures are unknown; or the supports are incomplete.)

How else is the Opinion Pattern different from the others? Well, for one thing, it may not be about a problem or a new idea. It can be frivolous or serious and the supporting reasons are more likely to express the author's personal point of view than present any verifiable data.

Essays are a classic form of the Opinion Pattern. Most bylined newspaper columns represent the opinions of the author. We even get "Commentary" on the evening TV news and the editorial page—a newsman's way of pointing out what is important in the jumble of facts that comes at us every day.

The Thesis Pattern—To prove something
Thesis
Proofs
Implications

Don't be intimidated by the word "thesis." Whenever you see someone expressing an original, controversial, or unproven idea and supporting it with solid facts, you are probably reading a Thesis Pattern piece. If the writer offers a significant answer to "So what?" you have a thesis.

A thesis can be profound or trivial, weighty or gossamer, valid or invalid. Most "important" nonfiction books, those landmark tomes that become classics—*The Silent Spring* by Rachel Carson or *The Female Eunuch* by Germaine Greer—are theses. They offer exciting new ways to look at generally known facts, or they provide a newly discovered piece of information that completely changes the accepted picture of something.

CHECK THIS OUT

Identify the Five Nonfiction Patterns

Now that you've analyzed the five nonfiction patterns, read the following short articles. Then match them with their formats. (Here is a helpful hint: An author's credit or byline on a newspaper story is a clue that the article may contain opinions and beliefs, rather than just facts.)

[A]
Lots of Fine Nursery Programs Being Offered

Three-year-old Rosario Cruz holds her tiny hammer tightly with both hands as she pounds earnestly on a nail-studded board. Around her, six other students at Middledale Nursery School are hammering, sawing, and sanding.

Rosario and her friends are just a few of the hundreds of youngsters who are enjoying the stimulation and socialization offered in the fourteen Central City nursery schools this year. Some of the schools have special programs like art, music, dancing, or gymnastics. Some are bilingual and some are church-sponsored. Here is a guide to four of them:

Middledale School is a co-ed nonsectarian school that emphasizes nonsexist role playing. Ages 2 yrs. 9 mos. to 5 yrs., 8 A.M.–6 P.M., Mon–Fri. $650/mo.

Wee Lassie School is operated by the St. Ignatius Convent and takes girls only. Emphasis is on arts and crafts. Ages 3–6, 9 A.M.–1 P.M., Mon–Fri. $110/mo.

Troll Hollow has a brightly painted store-front setting on Main St. Food is natural vegetarian and emphasis is on yoga, no-lose games, and community service projects. Ages 2 yrs. 6 mos.–6 yrs, 8:30 A.M.–5:30 P.M., Mon–Sat. $400/mo.

Essex Preparatory specializes in early reading and math skills. Ages 4–6 yrs, Mon-Wed-Fri, 9 A.M.–12:30 P.M. $325/mo.

[B]
Are Women the Best Carpenters?

Three-year-old Rosario Cruz holds her tiny hammer tightly with both hands as she pounds earnestly on a nail-studded board. Around her, six other students at Middledale Nursery School are hammering, sawing, and sanding.

These girls know subliminally what many are coming to believe today: that women make better carpenters than men.

Tests done last year at the University of Oslo on 1,003 men and 9,998 women showed that women scored an average of 11.1 points higher than men on spatial relation tests, a talent necessary for carpentry.

Women who have entered the advanced industrial trades program in the Central City Adult Education program in the past two years also did better than men. Of the 123 female students who began the program, 112 completed the 10 month program, a total of 92%. The 1,836 male students experienced only a 71% completion rate. Of the 112 females, 23 were in the top 5% of the graduation class, 64 were in the top 10%, and all were in the top 40%.

More and more, women are turning to carpentry as a natural outlet for their creativity.

A few years ago, women weren't considered strong enough to work a typewriter. Now, thanks to the changing customs, the hand that rocks the cradle may have made it first.

[C]
Last Happy Sounds As Funds Run Out

Three-year-old Rosario Cruz holds her tiny hammer tightly with both hands as she pounds earnestly on a nail-studded board. Around her, six other students at Middledale Nursery School are hammering, sawing, and sanding.

These children and 438 like them may soon have no place to play if the City Budget Commission fails to renew the sales tax that supports the city's 14 childcare centers.

"Most of these children would be left unattended," reports Phebe Garvin, chairman of the Save Our Nurseries Committee, "or their mothers will have to give up their jobs and accept public assistance because they cannot afford full-time childcare on their low salaries."

Budget Commissioner Diedrich Holmes sympathizes with the plight of the children, but reports that business resistance is high to a renewal of the sales tax: "Business was down 3% in the city last year, and they think the tax did it. They don't want it."

Ms. Garvin feels this is a shortsighted view. "Welfare rolls will cost the city much more than keeping the schools open."

Mayor Brinkley hopes that a solution can be found that will lower the sales tax and keep the centers open. "We are looking into a Sponsor Program that would let local businesses 'adopt' authorized charitable groups. . . ."

[D]
Making a Place for Hammer and Nails

Three-year-old Rosario Cruz holds her tiny hammer tightly with both hands as she pounds earnestly on a nail-studded board. Around her, six other students at Middledale Nursery School are hammering, sawing, and sanding.

Middledale is just one of many nursery schools in the state that have set up a carpentry corner. It sounds noisy, messy, and dangerous, but it needn't be if you follow a few simple procedures.

First, find an uncarpeted area and lay down Masonite if necessary to provide an impervious floor. Then make some low work tables. Sheets of 8 × 4–inch-thick plywood work well. Cut them in half and lay them on sturdy boxes or short-legged saw horses.

For each table, have two vises. Estimating the number of tools needed is more difficult, since most small children tend to "gang" around certain activities one day and ignore them the next. A good rule of thumb would be to have 4 hammers, 2 saws, and 2 hand drills for every 15 children in the school.

Finally, you will need a storage area for tools and wood. Try a wall pegboard with the tool outlines painted or drawn on so the children will be encouraged to return tools to the proper place. With a little planning, carpentry can be one of the most enjoyable parts of a nursery school program.

[E]
When Little Girls Do "Men's Work"

by Katharine Liu

Three-year-old Rosario Cruz holds her tiny hammer tightly with both hands as she pounds earnestly on a nail-studded board. Around her, six other students at Middledale Nursery School are hammering, sawing, and sanding.

Rosario and her classmates are learning more than manual skills and the pleasures of using tools. They are discovering that girls and boys can be equally talented (or awkward) at tasks that our society has assumed were male- or female-oriented.

Yet when they go on to public schools, they will discover the crushing burden of official discrimination. When Central High parents proposed that all shop classes be made co-educational, their greatest foes were the shop teachers themselves.

The cooking and sewing teachers said they didn't want boys clowning around near sharp scissors and hot stoves, while the metal and wood shop teachers painted equally bleak pictures of girls with burned or sawed-off fingers.

It would be nice to assume that our children can laugh off these preconceptions, but they are no less subject to peer pressure than we are.

Only when we assume that all men and women will be able to make cakes and bookcases, repair pants and plumbing, will we be free to escape the stereotypes that create low-paid "women's work" and high-paid "men's work."

PROBLEM ____________________

The problem is ____________________

The effect/s ____________________

The cause/s ____________________

The solution/s ____________________

THESIS ____________________

The thesis is ____________________

The proofs are ____________________

The implication is ____________________

OPINION ____________________

The opinion is ____________________

Reasons are ____________________

The significance is ____________________

INSTRUCTION ____________________

Step 1 ____________________

Step 2 ____________________

Step 3, etc. ____________________

INFORMATION ____________________

Facet 1 ____________________

Facet 2 ____________________

Facet 3, etc. ____________________

(*Answers are at the end of this chapter.*)

When you learn to spot the kind of nonfiction you are reading, you have a powerful tool for knowing what to look for and finding what you want in the toppling piles of print that threaten to drown us all.

IDENTIFYING HYBRIDS

Writers, like the rest of us, are not always perfect, so sometimes they create written works that are not "pure." For example, most autobiographies combine information and opinions.

Some journals like *The New York Times Magazine* favor problem/opinion articles. Some short problem pieces assume that you already know the causes or effects of the problem, and so don't mention them specifically. And then there are those pesky opinion pieces trying to masquerade as something else.

The five patterns are all related to each other:

INFORMATION = **facts**
facts + OPINION = THESIS
THESIS + **solution** = PROBLEM
solution = INSTRUCTION

Don't stop looking for patterns just because hybrids exist. If you're filing letters and run across one that could be filed two different ways, you can make a choice or you can photocopy it and put it in both files. The same goes for hybrids: Remember them both ways.

HUMOR AS A MEMORY AID

Edward de Bono says that God can't have a sense of humor because for Him there are no surprises. One of the chief ingredients of humor is an abrupt shift in pattern—an unexpected juxtaposition of elements or a "punch line." For example, the all-girls school that put on the musical *Seven Brides for Seven Brides*. Here's a real-life example, a press release from Playboy Enterprises concerning the wedding plans of Playboy founder Hugh Hefner.

> Hefner has requested that the ceremony and reception be kept as simple and private as possible. . . .
>
> Complete information on satellite feed times and coordinates will be provided several days before the ceremony by Independent Television News, which will be handling the video news release transmissions. In order to accommodate television stations and news bureaus wishing to have their own reporter at the Playboy Mansion, a fully equipped microwave van with camera and hand-held microphone will be available at the North Gates, 10236 Charing Cross Road, to transmit stand-up pieces to the reporters' base stations. . . .

DEEP READING

In *Information Anxiety*, Richard Saul Wurman says, "I believe diversions and distractions inspire our thinking."[7] He urges what he calls "deep thinking," a process that lets you wander through your mental forest, stopping and backtracking at will.

I want to urge you to engage in deep reading. Don't be afraid to stop reading so you can think about something that intrigues you. For instance, I ran across this fascinating statistic from the French magazine *L'Evenement du Jeudi:* "The average Frenchman uses 5.5 bars of soap a year; by comparison, the average American uses 11."

This led to the following train of thought about reasons for the discrepancy:

- French people are cleaner than Americans—they need less soap.
- Americans are cleaner than the French—they wash more often.
- The French use other cleaning agents besides soap.
- Soap is very expensive in France and therefore is not wasted.
- The French are thriftier than Americans.
- The French take more showers than Americans and therefore do not have their bars of soap melting in the bottom of the bathtub.
- Americans throw away soap bars when they get down to slivers.

- Americans do more manual labor and therefore need more soap to clean up at the end of the day.
- Americans use soap for purposes other than washing—for example, making soap sculptures or marking cloth for tailoring.

Even nonfiction reading can be as much about your own thought processes as the information on the printed page. Never be afraid to stop dead and go off in a trance, following your own thoughts to new insights and conclusions. The printed words will still be there when you get back, to recall or not as you choose.

ANSWERS

Humpty Dumpty Experiment II

The paragraph is about the difficulty of defining "intelligence" and how perceptions of it differ among different cultures. The author's opinion is that each culture perceives "intelligence" as the ability to cope with the culture's unique surroundings and needs, and tailors its children's education to meeting those needs.

What constitutes "intelligence" **varies** considerably from culture **to** culture, even among **groups** within a single **culture**. Obviously all parents **want** to prepare their **children** for maximum potential **intelligence/performance** in our difficult **world**. But which world? **Which** skills and talents **are** to be maximized **and** which ignored or **even** suppressed? Each cultural **group** teaches its children **to** respond as intelligently **as** possible to given **surroundings/situations**. When one group **decides/believes** that another is **less** intelligent or is "**too** smart for its **own** good," it is **trying** to judge it **by** its own standards. "**They** are N.L.U. (Not **Like** Us!)"

Humpty Dumpty Experiment III

Some possible answers are:

Great Britain: Why are they selling state-owned assets? What have they sold? Who bought what? How has this affected British citizens? What other countries are part of that $43 billion figure? What immediate benefits and long-term affects? Is the U.S. doing this? How will it affect my immediate and future life?

XYZ Company: What is the new address? If I don't use the old payment coupons, how should the payments be submitted? Starting with my next payment?

Lenin: What were Lenin's political beliefs? When and where was he persecuted? Did he flee Russia and come to America? What happened to him?

Humpty Dumpty Experiment IV

1. The first letter Z was shaped like a capital I or sword.
2. True, *zayin* was the seventh letter of the Hebrew alphabet.
3. The Romans used Z only in words of Greek origin.
4. Today the English call the letter "zed," while Italians and Spaniards say "zeta," but Americans pronounce it "zee."
5. Z reached English from Hebrew via Greek, Latin, and French.

Humpty Dumpty Experiment V

Progress
The sentence containing the main idea is sentence 4.
The sentences that support this idea are 5 and 6.

Stencils
The two main ideas are in sentence 1, supported by sentences 2, 3, and 4, and in sentence 5, supported by sentences 6 through 12.

Identify the Five Nonfiction Patterns

Problem—C
Problem: City childcare centers may lose funds and close.

Effects: Children will have no place to go.
Working mothers will need to quit their jobs to take care of their children.
Welfare roles will cost city more money than maintaining centers.
Cause: City Budget Commission will fail to renew supporting tax because business claims tax was cause of 3% business decline.
Solutions: Lower sales tax, but don't eliminate.
Develop sponsor program.

Thesis—B
Thesis: Women make better carpenters than men.
Proofs: Women scored higher on the University of Oslo's test.
Statistics from Central City program.
Implication: Female children should be encouraged to become carpenters.

Opinion—E
Opinion: Jobs should not be divided by sexes, and children should be encouraged to try all types of skills.
Reasons: Segregation is artificial and caused by peer pressure and lack of awareness.
Significance: Such discrimination is responsible for low-paying "women's jobs" and higher-paying "men's jobs."

Instruction—D
Step 1: Prepare working area.
Step 2: Provide proper equipment and materials.
Step 3: Set aside a storage area.

Information—A
Facet 1: Names of nursery programs available.
Facet 2: Specialties of each.
Facet 3: Requirements.
Facet 4: Schedules.
Facet 5: Cost.

DAY 7

How to Stretch Your Memory Capacity

WHAT YOU'LL LEARN IN THIS CHAPTER

- Exciting new discoveries about how the brain remembers
- Total-brain encoding for more efficient recall
- Your 100-Year Memory Warranty
- Handy everyday memory tricks
- The importance of *selective forgetting*

Is the mind a computer? Trying to explain the brain by comparing it to the hottest new technology has always been a popular pastime. Seventeenth-century Europeans visualized the brain as a lens and mirror, focusing thoughts and reflecting them back. In the nineteenth century, the brain became a giant factory powered by steam. Freud used this image when he described seething hidden forces that suddenly explode into action. The early twentieth century replaced the factory with telephones and radios that could send invisible electrical messages. Then the computer came along.

Of course the brain, with its seemingly infinite capabilities, has characteristics in common with nearly everything on Earth, including lenses, steam engines, telephones, and computers. But computers offer a good working analogy.

Computers can remember anything—or almost anything. Both computers and brains need input and produce output. Both have Random Access Memory, the ability to dip in anywhere in the storage area and assemble a whole from many parts. But so far computers have failed hilariously at translating one language to another, a feat that most five-year-olds in multilingual cultures have mastered. They also lack the ability to recognize the obvious, what people call "common sense." The one way a computer can usually (but not always) beat out humans is speed of recall.

Besides the ability to use language and common sense, you have one more consistent capacity that computers don't have: *Motivation!* You are in control of your own On/Off switch. A computer is lost without someone to tell it what to do and when to do it.

"I'd like to purchase some memory chips — one for frequently used numbers, another for people's names, and one for where I've put things."

A NEW LOOK AT THE BRAIN

Adventurers in the past thrilled the world as they explored remote jungles, icy poles, and even the surface of the moon. Some of today's explorers are charting an even more awesome terrain: the human brain. As our tools for observing and measuring brain activity become more sophisticated, some experts say our knowledge about the brain is doubling almost yearly!

One important discovery has been where and how the brain stores memory. Using a new tool called the positron emission tomography (PET) scan, brain researchers have been watching people think and remember. The PET scan shows the areas and intensity of brain activity as swiftly shifting, brightly colored patterns that look much like a TV weather map.

For many years, people thought that there were different places in the brain to store different kinds of memories and that each individual memory resided in a particular spot. However, people with severe brain injuries often retain extensive memory. They remember grammar rules, general cultural knowledge, such as what shoes and chairs are for, and they either remember all their close family members or none. No study could establish a particular locale for a particular kind of memory.

A new theory had to be developed to explain this: that a single memory is stored all over the brain. Until recently this had to remain just a theory. There was no way to prove or disprove it. But now, with the PET scan, we can actually watch the brain remember. In one experiment, volunteers were asked to recall specific words. The colored patterns that showed which parts of the brain were active lit up like Las Vegas at night, indicating that the volunteers were scanning much or all of their brains. The researchers concluded that the volunteers were locating, assembling, and confirming the information from a variety of sites: "Memory is like a piece of music—it has lots of different parts that come together to create a whole."[1] Other researchers have confirmed these findings in human and animal experiments.[2,3] The current scientific belief is that every memory is recorded throughout the brain.

USING ALL YOUR BRAIN

So what? you may be saying. Here's what. When we know where and how the brain remembers, we realize that the best way to remember anything is consciously to file it in as many ways as possible. This is why we can often remember the items on a shopping list that we've left behind: We noticed we were out of something. Maybe we had some discomfort when we could almost taste the item, reached for it, and found the box was empty. Then we had the kinesthetic experience of writing the word on paper. We looked at the written word, maybe said it aloud several times and went over it in our minds. (This is sometimes called "studying" or "rehearsing.") This memory was filed with most of our senses, giving us lots of ways to recall it.

Total-brain encoding ensures recall.

To encode information with your entire brain:

- Sort and classify the information in as many ways as you can.
- Make "multiple copies" by rehearsing the information in different ways—if one copy is lost, you will still have others.
- Give the information so much context, so many things that it relates to and reminds you of, that it can't be blocked by background noise.

CHECK THIS OUT

TOTAL-BRAIN ENCODING

Choose something you would like to remember and jot it down here. (Be more specific than "all the lyrics of Hammer" or "the Koran." Start more modestly.)

"I'd like to remember____
____."

Now encode that object or idea with *all* your brain.

- What does it look like? Sound like? Smell like? Taste like? Remind me of? (Wallow in the sensations.) If this is a person, imagine the feeling of shaking hands; the scent of cologne, soap, starch, or sweat; the sounds made when walking and speaking. If this is an idea, focus on how it makes you and others feel.
- Handle the object if possible or imagine a situation involving the idea: How does it feel to the touch? Rough, smooth, pleasant, unpleasant, painful?
- How important is it? How does it relate to other things, other experiences? Evaluate it. Is it good or bad, better or worse, bigger or smaller? How does it fit in the already established sequence of things? Does the sequence change because of it?
- Are you mad at it? Do you respond with happiness? Sorrow? Boredom? Jealousy? Anxiety?
- Are you curious about it? "Look at that!" "What if it . . . ?" "What if I . . . ?" "Could it also . . . ?" Interact with it.
- Write down the name or idea several times on another piece of paper. Look at what you have written.

You have now encoded the information using all your senses; you have evaluated it; have used verbal, visual, and kinesthetic memory; have responded emotionally; and have made yourself curious (or recognized your confusion or boredom).

Let's say that you are taking an art history class and feel as if you're drowning in unfamiliar names and terms. Start by singling out several artists that may be easy to confuse, say thirteenth-century Florentine painters Giotto and Cimabue or Flemish fifteenth-century painters Dürer, Cranach, and Holbein. If possible, find a portrait of each and react to it. Would you like to know this person? If no portrait exists, conjure your image of the kind of person who would produce these paintings. Now imagine meeting this artist in his working environment. Focus on the smells and sounds and sights. What is he wearing, eating? Who else is there? How do you respond to this place? Watch the artist working on one of the paintings you are supposed to remember. Is he in a frenzy of activity, muttering as paint splashes everywhere? Or is he serene, whistling to himself, making precise, small movements. Stare in your imagination at the painting and respond emotionally to it. What would you say if he asked for your opinion? How might he respond if you told him the truth? How does it compare to his other work? What questions would you want to ask this artist? Create a rap sheet for each artist with his name, vital statistics, and a list of his most famous works. Add your opinions and (important) the opinions of your art history professor. Then write down your own evaluation of the importance of this artist, both during his lifetime and in the years since.

The five or ten minutes you spend doing this will lock each painter as an individual into your memory. Like a computer, you have embedded information about him in all parts of your brain, ready for recall when any one of those fragments is activated. When you run across just one of the parts, your brain will immediately collect and recall all the others, using your powerful Random Access Memory.

YOUR 100-YEAR MEMORY WARRANTY

At one time or another, you've probably muttered about your occasional absentmindedness: "Oops, I must be getting senile." You meant it facetiously, but most likely there was a bit of black humor there, too. Well into this century, it was accepted that advancing age almost inevitably meant losing mental powers.

Fortunately we now know that most of the causes of mental decay are preventable or curable. Alzheimer's Disease has been identified as a specific, if so far irreversible, physical illness, distinct from mental malfunction caused by poor diet, stress, grief, isolation, certain medications, and depression. Dr. Gene Cohen, acting director of the National Institute on Aging, says that it is no longer a foregone conclusion that we will suffer mental deterioration when we get older: "Many of the changes that were said to be related to aging are now thought to be due to illness."[4]

How can you keep your recall sharp for the next hundred years? Obviously one way is to stay alive and healthy. Another method, more problematic, is to have a job where you are in charge. A survey of 2,720 elderly people in France found that the risk of memory loss was two or three times higher for farmers, domestic service employees, and blue-collar workers than it was for professionals or managers.[5] Of course, if you allow your mind to drift away right now, you can probably come up with a number of further questions for study, such as:

- Were those with memory loss exposed to more harmful environmental factors as a result of their work?
- Do people with stronger inborn memory skills tend to seek out professional and managerial careers?
- Could both gradual memory loss and career choices be dictated by heredity or cultural restrictions?
- Could the additional training and education that society often provides career-track children help maintain brain stimulation in later life? And if this is so, does "use it or lose it" apply to memory?

Memory training at any age makes a difference. Some researchers at the University of Utah set out to find what factors could improve recall among older people. They divided sixty seniors into four groups: Group 1 got memory training plus an incentive (reward); Group 2 got memory training only; Group 3 got a placebo "memory pill" plus an incentive; Group 4, as a control, got the placebo "memory pill" only. (Don't forget that placebos can have a powerful positive effect simply by focusing the participant on the task or process.)

These four groups were given word lists to recall. The first three groups were able to recall more words than the placebo-only group, but both of the groups that got training did better than the group that got only an incentive.[6] In experimental situations, outside rewards don't seem to improve memory. A Swedish researcher asked three groups of students to remember a list of words. The first group got no instructions and was offered no reward. The second was told—after they had looked at the words but before they tried to recall them—that there would be a cash reward. The third group was told about the reward before they saw the words. All groups scored about the same.[7] The inference is that training your memory gets better results than trying to bribe yourself into remembering.

Several training programs that focus on older people have begun in Europe. In France, a pension fund is sponsoring a workshop called *Eureka!*, meant for people over fifty-five. Its popularity has already generated similar programs, including another in France called *Agora* (Greek for "marketplace"). *Agora* began as memory workshops for retired people, but soon expanded into "cerebral fitness" seminars for corporate employees.

A participant in a *Eureka!* program attends fifteen weekly two-hour sessions with trained counselors. At a typical session, twenty to twenty-five people sit around a large table, reviewing the week's news, solving brain teasers, and doing memory games. Some samples from both programs are:

- Find a relationship between two unrelated images projected on a screen—a suitcase and a belt or a comb and a fork. Come up with a way to connect and recall them, such as a verbal phrase, their size, use, or what they are made of.
- Copy a geometric design seen briefly. Then draw it in reverse.
- "What do a ship and a broom have in common?"
- "What synonyms are there for poet?"
- "Name some antonyms for reality."
- "How many kinds of government can you name?"

"This is to stimulate curiosity and communication with others," says psychologist Jocelyne de Rotrou, who designed the *Eureka!* program. "The exercises involve all the mental faculties: perception, concentration, reasoning, speech, imagination. [Older] people often register poorly [on memory because] they do not focus or concentrate. But training can restore those abilities." Françoise Forette, Director of the Fondation Nationale de Gérontologie in Paris, says, "We have found that [after memory training] older people gain in other areas: in reasoning, in judgment, and in analysis."[8]

BRAIN TRAINING

Now, while you're still young(er), is the time to train yourself to notice, observe, focus, file, and be eager to remember. So far, all research indicates that mental exercises maintain and expand recall. Numerous studies have shown that connective tissue in the brains of animals increases when they are intellectually stimulated, indicating that they may be able to think more efficiently afterward. One cautious 54-year-old scientist feels that so far, there is "no specific and direct human evidence," but even he recommends keeping mentally active.[9]

CHECK THIS OUT

MENTAL AEROBICS

Give yourself memory exercises every day. As with any successful exercise program, you will only keep it up if you frame your efforts as something fun and self-enhancing, showing both immediate and long-term results. Start today by memorizing a poem you like or the batting scores of a favorite player or all the lyrics of a favorite song. Recite all the streets you cross in your typical daily traffic pattern. Notice someone nearby, glance away, and recall as much as you can of what he or she is wearing. Recall the names of all your schoolteachers, starting in kindergarten. Devise recall games for idle moments.

Here are some more observation and recall exercises.

An Observation Exercise

1. If you wear shoes with laces, how many lace holes are in each shoe? (Don't peek.)
2. What was the last thing you said aloud prior to this exact moment?
3. Summon up a mental image of the person nearest and dearest to you. On which side is his or her hair parted? Are his or her earlobes attached at the bottom or do they hang slightly separate from the cheek? What was s/he wearing the last time you saw her/him?
4. Without looking—does your watch have Arabic or Roman numerals? Does it have all the numbers or just 12, 3, 6, and 9? (If your watch is digital, substitute your favorite clock.)
5. On the $5 bill, does Abraham Lincoln face left or right?

A Visualizing Exercise

Think of the name of a friend or famous person. Shut your eyes and fix the words on the blackboard of your mind. When you can see the name clearly, spell it backward. If you are doing this successfully, you will lose track of what the original name was and actually be reading a "nonsense" word off the blackboard. As soon as this becomes easy to do, use longer and longer words.

A Listening Exercise

Listen to a sentence on the radio or TV. Turn the sound down immediately and fix the sentence in your mind. Then say it backward to yourself. Start with short sentences and work up. (It may help to "write" the sentence on a mental blackboard so you can "read" it backward.)

Your Trunk of Memory Tricks

Before the written word, all knowledge was passed on verbally. People had to rely on memory for everything they knew, their entire cultural history. In some parts of the world, there are still skilled individuals who can recite genealogies, community records, and religious texts for hours from memory. On a much more modest level, we all learn or contrive mnemonic devices every day for everyday tasks. The ones we remember best are usually funny, often naughty, and frequently rhymed. Some examples are:

Calendar

Thirty days hath September,
April, June, and November.
All the rest have thirty-one.
Excepting February alone,
Which hath but twenty-eight, in fine,
Till leap year gives it twenty-nine.
(Common in the New England states)

Fourth, eleventh, ninth, and sixth,
Thirty days to each affix.
Every other thirty-one,
Except the second month alone.
(Common among the Friends community in Pennsylvania)

Spelling

I before E
Except after C
Or when sounded like A
As in "neighbor" or "weigh."
(Exceptions: Neither leisured foreigner seized the weird heights.)

Desert has one S because we always want less.
Dessert has two S's because we always want more.

Always eat a PIEce of PIE.

Scientific

Little Chilies Taste Very Pungent. (Sections of Pascal computer language: labels, constants, types, variables, procedures)

C. HOPKINS (The symbols for the eight most common elements in seawater: C—carbon, H—hydrogen, O—oxygen, P—phosphorous, K—potassium, I—iodine, N—nitrogen, S—sulfur)

"Papa's eating off my plate," protested Roger. (Geological epochs of the Cenozoic Era: Paleocene, Eocene, Oligocene, Miocene, Pliocene, Pleistocene, Recent)

Historical

In fourteen-hundred-ninety-two
Columbus sailed the ocean blue.

Medical

When the face is red, raise the head.
When the face is pale, raise the tail.
(Red Cross first aid instructions)

On old Olympus's towering top,
A fat-assed German vaults and hops.
(Memorable medical student vulgarity for recalling the twelve cranial nerves: olfactory, optic, oculomotor, trochlear, trigeminal, abducents, facial, acoustic, glossopharyngeal, vagus, spinal accessory, hypoglossal. Despite attempts to introduce a more decorous and informative mnemonic, this one has stuck.)

The Wrong-Wrist Trick: A variation on the string around the finger. If a thought crosses your mind about something you must do later and you're not in a position to write it down, switch your watch to the other wrist. This is a good way to recall something you must do before leaving home or the office, since, by habit, we always seem to glance at our wristwatch during periods of transition. A variation is to switch a ring from one finger to another. The constant nagging sense of something different will help cue what you want to recall.

The Pin-It-On Trick: If you don't wear a watch or you want to remember several things, try a safety pin in a highly visible or inconvenient place—the cuff of your shirt, the zipper pull of your briefcase or purse. You may feel ridiculous, but it beats arriving at the airport or theater without your ticket, or leaving the coffeemaker on all weekend. In the privacy of your own home, you can even pin a large note to your chest or cuff with the phone number you must call in two hours. Very hard to forget!

The Displaced-Furniture Trick: Changing something in your environment can provide memory cues for what you want to remember later. If you must call someone the very first thing in the morning, when you are usually groggy and forgetful, set the telephone (if the cord is long enough) on the toilet seat. Or put a chair across the bedroom doorway so you have to climb over it. These physical cues will remind you of the important call. If an idea comes to you in the shower, toss a plastic shampoo bottle out onto the bathroom floor. Nearly asleep when you remember something you want to recall the next day? Throw a pillow where you will step on it the next morning, or tip the lamp shade, or pull the nightstand drawer halfway out, or set the clock on the floor. If you're on the phone and there's something you must do as soon as you hang up, lay a chair over sideways or dump your pencil jar out on the desk or put any object in a strange position. It will be hard to forget after you hang up. Crammed in a commuter train? Button your coat wrong or hold a coin in your fist until you get off. Any disruption of the ordinary can provide a memory cue.

The Sign Trick: Tape big signs or stick Post-its on telephones, doors, mirrors, steering wheels, television and computer screens, reminding yourself about tasks and appointments. Put the sign where it will keep you from using the object. Warning: Any sign that stays in one place too long becomes part of the scenery and is ignored.

The Underfoot Trick: If there's something you must take with you when you leave, set it on the floor where you'll have to step on it to go out the door, or hang it from the doorknob in a way that will make it awkward to open the door. (Not advisable in high-traffic locations, but often useful at home.) Warning: As above, familiarity destroys cue value.

The Piggyback Trick: Attach new or temporary tasks to something you already do on a similar schedule. Rubber band medication bottles to your toothbrush. When you go to brush your teeth, you'll remember to take your pills. Anything you use regularly—toilet seats, dog leashes, mirrors, shower heads, cars, coffeepots, refrigerator door handles, hairbrushes, razors—can be piggybacked with your need-to-recall activity.

The Egg-Carton Trick: This works great for change and for medication. If you have a complex medication schedule—one pill three times a day, one once a day, one twice a day, etc.—line them up in a topless egg carton. Write the days of the week above each cup on the long side and the times of day beside each horizontal row.

You can set several cartons together to create three or four cups per day and seven days per week. Simply dole out the pills for the week into the appropriate cups. You'll know immediately whether you remembered to take your morning dosage because the cup will be full or empty. No more missing medication or dangerously doubling the dosage. The egg carton system also works superbly for having the right change on hand. If you routinely need a certain amount in coins in specific denomi-

nations for carfare, tolls, parking meters, or vending machines, mark the egg cups appropriately and put the right coins in each slot. Then make it a habit to grab the coins each morning as you leave the house, or each Tuesday when you need quarters for the washing machine, and to reload the egg carton each Sunday. A great way to handle kids' lunch money and school expenses.

The Personalize-It Trick: Here are some personalized memory aids which may inspire you to create your own. Shawn puts empty tape dispensers, staple boxes, burned-out light bulbs, and dead batteries in her purse so she won't forget to replace them when she goes to the market. John, a very logical person, uses the "First Principle" and puts everything in the best, most logical place. Then, he says, if he can't find something, he simply rebuilds the chain of logic and there it is: "Do it the best way first and it will be obvious." Joan has a last-minute-check rhyme for leaving the house, "Cash, keys, IDs," and an acronym for leaving the country, "PATTI," for passport, travelers' checks, ticket. A forgetful friend in New York keeps a spare key on top of an air conditioner ledge around the corner from his apartment. It's above eyesight, but he stops to check if it is still there every week or so. Charlene found two similarly named movie theaters near her house confusing until she created a mnemonic: The Coliseum (with an l) is on Clement (also with an l), while the Coronet (with an r) is on Geary (also with an r). She immediately stopped turning up at one for a film showing ten blocks away at the other. Eleanor had trouble remembering the sequence of streets in her new neighborhood—Jones, Taylor, Mason, Powell—until she realized they formed the acronym JUMP with U replacing the T in Taylor. All of these personalized mnemonics are silly, and all work *because* they are personal.

The Do-It-Now Trick: When you think of something you have to do, do it. Lay out the book you have to take back to the library, write the check, lock the door. Now, not later.

The Ask-a-Friend Trick: Say, "Roger, would you remind me to check the washer in ten minutes?" Hearing yourself say the words is a good memory aid. Advantages: You have someone else to blame when you both forget. Disadvantages: You may lose Roger as a friend.

The Simplify-Your-Life Trick: Remember boring everyday things outside your head. Use (really use) calendars, diaries, address books, lists. Save your in-head memory for the good stuff. Trick, charm, coerce, and cajole yourself into developing those life-enhancing structures called "habits" for handling the trivia of life. Don't be a slave to the misplaced, overlooked, and forgotten. If the old adage "A place for everything and everything in its place" sounds unbearably oppressive, consider all the time and energy that is wasted on turmoil and regret. Free yourself for recalling the important things in life.

CHECK THIS OUT

Total-Brain Encoding Revisited

Remember the thing you decided to remember in the *Total-Brain Encoding* exercise on page 173? Can you recall it now? Probably, but if not, go back and review it again. Retracing strengthens the memory patterns in your mind.

American Presidents Revisited

It is now several days at least since you first tried the linking of American presidents in Day 3. Stop now and run through the list in your head. If you are still stuck in spots, go back and review. Are you suitably impressed by how well you can recall them?

You have worked very hard, learned a lot, and hopefully had some fun. From time to time, go back and review the skills and memory systems in this book that you have decided are relevant to your current life. Occasionally glance at those you have discarded—they may suddenly seem appealing and useful.

Here's to your exciting new rapid memory.

NOTES

Day 1 Your One-Minute Memory Manager

1. Richard Saul Wurman, *Information Anxiety*, New York: Doubleday, 1989, p. 149.
2. A. R. Luria, *The Mind of a Mnemonist*, trans. Lynn Solotaroff, Cambridge: Harvard University Press, chapters 1–3. On synesthesia, pp. 21–22.
3. Edward de Bono, *De Bono's Thinking Course*, New York: Facts on File Publications, 1985 edition, p. 83.
4. Dr. Samuel Johnson, from Boswell's *Life of Johnson*, "Epitaph on Goldsmith," June 22, 1776.
5. Wurman, p. 54.
6. Wurman, p. 7.

Day 2 How Your Memory Works

1. Robert J. Sternberg, *The Triarchic Mind*, New York: Viking, 1988, pp. 119–120.
2. Robert Ornstein and David Sobel, *The Healing Brain*, New York: Simon and Schuster, 1987, p. 105.

3. Beth Livermore, "Build a Better Brain," *Psychology Today*, September/October 1992, pp. 40–47, citing work of Marcus Raichle, Ph.D., of Washington University in St. Louis, and Larry Squire, Ph.D., of Veteran's Affairs Medical Center, San Diego.
4. de Bono, p. 35.
5. Sternberg, p. 18.
6. Eleanor Rosch Heider, "Universals of Color Naming and Memory," *Journal of Experimental Psychology*, April 1972, pp. 10–20.
7. Alan Baddeley, "Working Memory," *Science*, January 31, 1992, pp. 556–559.
8. Endel Tulving, "Episodic and Semantic Memory," in *Organization of Memory*, edited by Endel Tulving and Wayne Donaldson, New York: Academic Press, 1972.
9. Jonathan W. Schooler and James W. Tanaka, "Composites, Compromises, and CHARM: What is the evidence for blend memory representations?" University of Pittsburgh Learning Research & Development Center, *Journal of Experimental Psychology* 102(1):96–100, March 1991.
10. Maggie Bruck at McGill University and Stephen Ceci at Cornell University, "Suggestibility of the Child Witness: An Historical Review and Synthesis," in *Psychological Bulletin* 113(3):403–439, May 1993.
11. Reported by Reuters, *San Francisco Chronicle*, August 11, 1993.
12. Ulric Neisser and Robert W. Beckland at Cornell University, "Selective Looking: Attempting to Visually Specify Event," *Cognitive Psychology* 7(4):480–494, October 1975.
13. E. W. Russell and M. E. D'Hollosy, Veterans' Affairs Medical Center, Miami, FL, "Memory and attention," *Journal of Clinical Psychology* 48(4):530–538, July 1992.
14. Eric Berne, M.D., *The Structure and Dynamics of Organizations and Groups*, New York: Grove Press, 1966, p. 153.
15. H. D. Kruse, chairman, and Russell Wilder, "Principles underlying studies of nutritional pertinence to the influence of supplements on growth, physical fitness, and health," *Archive of Internal Medicine* 74:258–279, October 1944; and Phyllis Wittman and Russell Wilder, "Investigations of human requirements for B-Vitamins," Section 5: Psychological observations, *Bulletin of the National Research Council* 116:89, June 1948.

Day 3 How to Master Memory Systems

1. Richard Bandler, *Using Your Brain—for a Change*, Moab, UT: Real People Press, 1985, p. 121.
2. Harry Lorayne, *Harry Lorayne's Page-a-Minute Memory Book*, New York: Ballantine Books, New York, 1985, p. 16.

Day 4 How to Remember Names

1. In a comedy routine aired on MTV. (Warfield played Roz on *Night Court.*)
2. *Million Dollar Legs* was a delightful 1932 Paramount musical starring W. C. Fields, Lyda Roberti, Jack Oakie, Susan Fleming (later the wife of Harpo Marx), and cross-eyed silent film comedian Ben Turpin.
3. A. Wahlin, L. Backman, T. Mantyla, A. Herlitz, M. Viitanen, and B. Winblad, Section of Psychology, Stockholm Gerontology Research Center, "Prior knowledge and face recognition in a community-based sample of healthy, very old adults," *Journal of Gerontology* 48(2):54–61, March 1993.

Day 5 How to Remember Dates and Numbers

1. Luria, pp. 31, 32, 59.
2. Luria, p. 59.
3. T. R. Reid, "The Man Who Loves Numbers," *Washington Post*, reprinted in the *San Francisco Chronicle*, July 17, 1989.
4. Gregor W. Pinney, "Memory whiz shows off his slice of pi," *Minneapolis-St. Paul Star Tribune*, reprinted in the *San Francisco Examiner*, July 29, 1993.
5. J. Jacobs, "Experiments in 'Prehension,' " *Mind* (1887), pp. 75–82.
6. K. Anders Ericsson and William G. Chase, "Exceptional Memory," *American Scientist*, November/December 1982, pp. 607–615.
7. R. D. Hill, S. L. Schwob, and S. Ottman, "Self-generated mnemonics for number recall in young and old adults," Department of Educational Psychology, University of Utah, Salt Lake City, *Perceptual Motor Skills* 76(2):467–490, April 1993.

Day 6 How to Remember What You Read

1. Wurman, p. 45.
2. Franklin J. Agardy, Ph.D. (President, Evelyn Woods Speed Reading Dynamics, Inc.), *How to Read Faster and Better*, New York: Simon & Schuster, Inc., 1981, p. 89.
3. Doris Lessing, *The Golden Notebook*, New York: Simon & Schuster, 1962, pp. xviii–xix.
4. R. K. Wagner and R. J. Sternberg, "Executive controls in reading comprehension," in *Executive Control Processes in Reading*, edited by B. Britton & S. M. Glynn, Hillsdale, NJ: Erlbaum, 1987.
5. de Bono, p. 42.

6. Quoted by Hubert L. Dreyfus and Stuart E. Dreyfus in *Mind Over Machine,* New York: Macmillan, The Free Press, 1986, p. 60.
7. Wurman, p. 42.

Day 7 How to Stretch Your Memory Capacity

1. Livermore, citing Marcus Raichle, Ph.D. and Larry Squire, Ph.D.
2. Livermore, about a group led by Larry Squire, Ph.D.
3. Gina Kolata in "Mental Gymnastics," *The New York Times Magazine*, October 6, 1991, pp. 15–17, 42, 44, reports the research of Zaven Khachaturian, Associate Director for the Neuroscience and Neuropsychology of Aging at the National Institute on Aging, who found that when he gave a cat something to look at, both the visual and audio centers of the brain showed stimulation.
4. Kolata, p. 42.
5. J. F. Dartigues, M. Gagnon, J. M. Mazaux, P. Barberger-Gateau, D. Commenges, L. Letenneur, and J. M. Orgogozo, "Occupation during life and memory performance in nondemented French elderly community residents," *Neurology* 42(9):1697–1701, September 1992.
6. Robert D. Hill, Martha Storandt, and Claudia Simeone, University of Utah, *Journals of Gerontology* 45(6):227–232, November 1990.
7. Alan Baddeley, *Your Memory: A User's Guide*, New York: Macmillan, 1982, p. 30, citing a study by Lars Gören Nillson in *Personal communication* (no date).
8. Marlise Simons reporting in "Le Brain Jogging," *The New York Times Magazine*, October 6, 1991, pp. 16, 44.
9. Zaven Khachaturian, associate director for the Neuroscience and Neuropsychology of Aging at the National Institute on Aging, as reported by Gina Kolata in "Mental Gymnastics," *The New York Times Magazine*, October 6, 1991.

INDEX